# Real-Time Decisions

**Educators Using
FORMATIVE ASSESSMENT
to Change Lives NOW!**

# Real-Time Decisions

## Educators Using FORMATIVE ASSESSMENT to Change Lives NOW!

### KRISTIN ANDERSON

LEAD+
LEARN
PRESS

ENGLEWOOD, COLORADO

The Leadership and Learning Center
317 Inverness Way South, Suite 150
Englewood, Colorado 80112
Phone 1.866.399.6019 | Fax 303.504.9417
www.LeadandLearn.com

Published by Lead + Learn Press, a division of Advanced Learning Centers, Inc.

Library of Congress Cataloging-in-Publication Data

Anderson, Kristin R.
  Real-time decisions : educators using formative assessment to change lives now! / Kristin Anderson.
    p. cm.
  Includes bibliographical references.
  ISBN 978-1-935588-13-9 (alk. paper)
  1. Educational tests and measurements—United States—Case studies. 2. Academic achievement—United States—Case studies. 3. Educational evaluation—United States—Case studies. I. Title.
  LB3051.A6975 2011
  371.26—dc23

                                                        2011021469

ISBN 978-1-935588-13-9

Printed in the United States of America

15  14  13  12  11      01  02  03  04  05  06  07

# Contents

# About the Author

 **Kristin R. Anderson** began her career as a high school English teacher for students who were kicked out of Denver Public Schools. Since then, she has worked in multiple K–12 settings in various instructional and administrative roles, and has obtained advanced degrees from Sterling College in Kansas, the University of Denver, and the University of Colorado in Colorado Springs. She is a longtime student of the field, a passionate educator, and an inspirational leader. Kristin is the author of *Data Teams Success Stories, Volume 1,* and currently serves as Senior Director of Professional Learning with The Leadership and Learning Center in Englewood, Colorado. She resides in Castle Rock, Colorado, with her husband of thirteen years and two children.

# Acknowledgments

Thank you to the following people who made this book happen, for taking the initiative to make formative assessment a priority, responding to student and teacher needs real time, and sharing your journey with all of us.

- B. R. Jones—Supervising Principal, Wayne County High School, Waynesboro, Mississippi

- Brett Gies—Superintendent, Sioux County Schools, Harrison, Nebraska

- Lauren Campsen—Principal, Ocean View Elementary School, Norfolk Public School District, Norfolk, Virginia

- William "Tommy" Thompson—Principal, New London High School, New London Public Schools, New London, Connecticut

- Stephanie Deroam—Teacher, Austin Parkway Elementary School, Fort Bend Public School District, Sugar Land, Texas

- Derrick Cameron—Principal, Macklin School, Living Sky School Division, Macklin, Saskatchewan, Canada

- Jo Peters—Principal, Lew Wallace Elementary School, Albuquerque Public Schools, Albuquerque, New Mexico

- Bill Hogan—Assistant Superintendent of Schools, Carroll County Public Schools, Carrollton, Kentucky

- Hope Stuart—Principal, Berea Elementary School, Valley Central School District, Montgomery, New York

- Tracey Vianden—Special Education Teacher, Berea Elementary School, Valley Central School District, Montgomery, New York

Thank you as well to the many courageous educators behind these real-time decisions: team members, the schools' support staff members, and the administrations that made brave decisions to invest in professional development, monitor implementation, and champion the process throughout.

Finally, thank you to my two beautiful children, Lauren and Evan Anderson. It is a privilege to be your mom and guide you, as God continues to grow you into the persons He created you to be! You continue to amaze, challenge, inspire, encourage, and love me—real time.

# Introduction

The phrase "real time" has become part of our 21st-century lifestyle and vernacular. We have access to real-time stock quotes, Web casts, videos, GPS tracking, seismograms, sports, concerts, blogs, Tweets, Facebook updates, weather, scores, computing, gaming, flight monitoring, radio, bidding, leads, and warehousing. *Real Time with Bill Maher* is a current television show, physicians are using real-time radiology to locate and immediately treat certain types of cancers, and some people even spend their time at www.usdebtclock.org tracking the accumulation of the national debt in real time.

Recently I discovered if I texted the word "Broncos" to 66916, I would receive real-time updates regarding everything that happens within the Denver Broncos franchise. When a score is made during a game, I am alerted. When they cut an old player, recruit a new one, or fire a coach, I am there (given their performance over the past few years, I have been "there" many times). With this instant information, I feel in the know and empowered even though I have absolutely no ability to influence the information I am provided.

"Real time" has been defined as referring to something that occurs immediately or instantaneously. In the world of computing, real-time operating systems are required to respond as rapidly as required by the user, or necessitated by the process being utilized. When they function as designed, there are no noticeable delays.

What if our schools and districts took on the essentials of computer operating systems? What if we responded to our students' educational needs as rapidly as necessary? What if students received on-the-spot feedback that assisted them in reaching and exceeding standards?

Formative assessments allow educators to operate in the mode of real-time decision making. They take place while the learning is occurring, and in the field of education, it is difficult to get any more "real time" than that.

There is a tremendous body of research to support the use of formative assessment, and while the articles and books vary, there are key terms that appear frequently across multiple texts. Formative assessments:

- Are diagnostic, active, and transformative
- Provide regular and descriptive feedback
- Supply status reports on current learning

• Empower educators to design, adjust, alter, develop, shape, mold, and differentiate

• Offer opportunity, encouragement, support, improvement, motivation, and growth

James Popham defines formative assessment in the following way: *"Formative assessment is a planned process in which assessment-elicited evidence of students' status is used by teachers to adjust their ongoing instructional procedures, or by students to adjust their current learning-tactics"* (Popham, 2008).

The acronym R.E.A.L. further defines and highlights the real-time capabilities of formative assessment:

**R**igorous—Formative assessments should be designed to monitor student progress toward the mastery of their given grade-level standards. Therefore, even if a student reads or writes below grade level, they are consistently exposed to the texts and objectives that match the expectations of their age. This practice, combined with deep remediation and infusion of necessary skills, has been proven to move students who struggle to meet the desired outcomes.

**E**ffective—The research is in. Formative assessments have made, and continue to make, a dramatic impact on student achievement!

In a late-1990s review of 250 empirical studies of classroom assessment that were drawn from 680 published investigations, Paul Black and Dylan Wiliam asserted, *"The research reported here shows conclusively that formative assessment does improve learning"* (Black and Wiliam, 1998).

In a 2005 OECD publication, *Formative Assessment: Improving Learning in Secondary Classrooms*, an analysis of eight case studies asserted, *"Formative assessment—the frequent assessments of student progress to identify learning needs and shape teaching—has become a prominent issue in education reform. The achievement gains associated with formative assessment have been described as 'among the largest ever reported for educational interventions'."*

In his 2009 publication titled *Visible Learning*, John Hattie created a synthesis of over 800 meta-analyses relating to achievement to determine what is working (and what isn't working) in education. Through his research, he found formative assessment has an effect size of $d=0.90$ and ongoing feedback of student performance has a $d=0.73$ effect (almost three times the average effect size). Note, Hattie defines desired effects as those above $d=0.40$, which are attributable to the specific interventions or methods being researched.

**A**ssessment *for* Learning—Assessments can be grouped into two categories: Assessment *of* learning is summative (end-of-unit, end-of-quarter, or end-of-year assessments). Generally, the information from these types of tests is obtained after the learning occurs, and it is too late to make any midcourse corrections necessary to ensure success. Assessment *for* learning is formative (synonyms include productive, constructive, and influential) and can be comprised of Common Formative Assessments, Performance Assessments, exit slips, journaling, Q and A, and so on.

The second type of assessments, or assessments *for* learning, are designed to give the teacher and student immediate information regarding the student's mastery of the targeted objective or outcome. This data is then used to modify lessons within an intended unit of instruction to ensure the needs of all learners are met (from those who have demonstrated proficiency to those who have a long way to go).

The practices embedded into assessments for learning build student confidence and educator strategy. As Rick Stiggins once stated, *"In short, the effect of assessment for learning, as it plays out in the classroom, is that students keep learning and remain confident they can continue to learn at productive levels if they keep trying to learn. In other words, students don't give up in frustration or hopelessness"* (Stiggins, 2002).

**L**eading—Schools and districts that choose to embed a formative assessment process into their instructional routines are leading the way when it comes to extraordinary student achievement and high-performing cultures. Students and their instructors lead their peers with the use of empowered practices that elevate teaching and learning to the professional status it demands. As Sadler illustrates about the formative assessment process, *"Teachers use feedback to make programmatic decisions with respect to readiness, diagnosis and remediation. Students use it to monitor the strengths and weaknesses of their performances, so that aspects associated with success or high quality can be recognised and reinforced and unsatisfactory aspects modified or improved"* (Sadler, 1989).

The book you are about to read is a collection of the real-time decisions made by your peers in the industry. They are ordinary people—central office administrators, principals, and teachers—many of whom have never written a newspaper or magazine article, let alone a chapter in a book. However, even though they may be underpublished, they are models for all of us, and their stories are so compelling they will leave you in awe. These leaders are driven to live and practice as though every moment in the classroom matters, and they have a true passion to address the immediate needs of their learners and respond as rapidly as required.

The reflection pages that immediately follow each story are titled "Getting Real." They serve as a venue for you to process the messages, deliberate practices, and courageous decisions of each school or district represented in this book, as they implemented the process of formative assessment. Feel free to write, draw, and plan on these pages and consume this publication; use them as a tool to help you refine, construct, and form or enhance your assessment point of view.

Most importantly, no matter where you are at in your assessment journey, there is something in this book for you. These decisions take place in urban, suburban, and rural schools and districts. They can serve as models for introducing formative assessment into your setting, supply exemplars for system-wide implementation, or provide a few tips to help you refine your current best practices. Regardless of your needs and situation, this book will allow you to formatively evaluate your current assessment status and use the data to drive your decision making—real time!

# CHAPTER ONE

# Wayne County High School
## Waynesboro, Mississippi

*"Once it was understood that formative assessment was to be used to make real-time decisions about instruction (before instruction began, during instruction, and even after instruction), the staff began to feel more comfortable about the process. . . . The amazing transformation here was that after a short while, the culture transformed from one of defending territory, to one of working for the common good. . . . In many ways, Common Formative Assessments have changed the way of thinking about educating students at Wayne County High School."*

—B. R. Jones, Supervising Principal

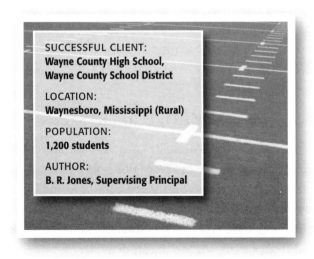

SUCCESSFUL CLIENT:
**Wayne County High School,
Wayne County School District**

LOCATION:
**Waynesboro, Mississippi (Rural)**

POPULATION:
**1,200 students**

AUTHOR:
**B. R. Jones, Supervising Principal**

# DEMOGRAPHICS

Wayne County High School (WCHS) is a rural school located in southeast Mississippi serving approximately 1,200 students in grades 9 through 12. The school serves a population of students who are 60 percent African American and 40 percent Caucasian. With 80 percent of the students eating free or reduced lunch, it is safe to say that poverty abounds. Most parents work in the timber industry, the oilfield, or have small farms. The manufacturing jobs have long been shipped overseas.

The high school was formed in 1989 when four smaller schools were merged to form one county high school to serve the approximately 26,000 residents of Wayne County. At the outset there was great angst about the decision to close the outer high schools and combine into what some would consider an impersonal conglomerate. The saving grace would appear to be the success that has been found in athletics from this merger. In 2001, specifically in football and girls' basketball, all of Wayne County found new reason to get excited as the high school would go on to represent the county and the various communities in several state championships. This has brought great notoriety to the school and developed a deep sense of pride in the community and the school.

Unfortunately, another change began to take place: the school was getting the reputation for being unsafe. With several high-profile fights where the local authorities had to be called in and many students were forced to leave the school due to disciplinary action, it was apparent that a change had to be made in leadership. This change came in August 2007. Three days before students were to report to school, another principal was appointed. Many changes were made to the everyday routines of the school that led to drastic reductions in disruptive behavior. A new vision was also set toward improving student learning and, most importantly, making data-driven decisions.

# PRE-FORMATIVE ASSESSMENT

In the first days of the administrative change, it was made apparent that the focus of all that Wayne County High School did from this point forward would be directed at improving student achievement. The administration would build on the success of the athletic teams and seek to instill the same enthusiasm for high performance in math, science, and language arts. These changes would be directed at implementing research-based strategies for improving student achievement.

A look inside the school saw a great teaching staff that had sanctimoniously taken a backseat to the pride that had been generated by the athletic teams. Classroom instruction was fragmented, as one might expect in most high schools in the

United States. Teachers taught from textbooks pretty much in lockstep, knowing that the state standards documents existed, but still relying on what they had most readily available.

The administration needed to create engagement with the staff and provide them with opportunities to take control of the instructional process. Student performance had been on a decline for the past three years, and no one really cared to ask why. One of the main issues came to light quickly: morale was low due to the discipline issues that plagued the school. Immediately, the administration went to work to create a safe and secure learning environment. With major changes in supervision schedules and duty assignments, within a semester the fights were a thing of the past. The change was incredible. Some teachers describe the change as miraculous.

Since the discipline issues were curbed, it was time to turn the eyes of educators toward the lagging student achievement scores. This same year, the state of Mississippi changed the accountability system so that no longer would the state's schools be compared to one another with accountability ratings; rather the schools in Mississippi would be compared with schools nationwide. In addition, the standards were raised exponentially in the new standards documents for math and language arts that came out in 2007 for the state of Mississippi (Mississippi Department of Education, 2007). This in and of itself led to a need to look closely at the common practices that were taking place at Wayne County High School.

We had all heard about the fact that we needed to be data driven, but no one on the WCHS staff could really define what that meant. Data in the form of state tests and college entrance exams are readily available, but those are one-shot assessments; once the student has taken the test, there is very little that can be done to improve student knowledge and skill. There had to be a way to assess students and have this data available to help guide instruction on a weekly basis. The answer was to develop Common Formative Assessments.

## STEPS TO COMMON FORMATIVE ASSESSMENTS

The first consideration in developing Common Formative Assessments must be the curriculum that is intended to be taught. More importantly, the key is determining a focus in this design to make sure that it can be taught to students in the time allotted. Robert Marzano, in his book *What Works in Schools: Translating Research into Action* (2003), called this a "Guaranteed and Viable" curriculum. The guarantee relates to the fact that regardless of what classroom the students are assigned to, they will have the opportunity to learn the content. The viability of the curriculum refers to the time that the student has to interact with this content. According to Marzano's research, if a school system were to cover all of the standards in all of the standards documents that have been articulated for students to learn, then the span of schooling would have to be extended from K through 12 to K through 22 (Marzano, 2003). At Wayne County High School, the first step in developing Common Formative Assessments was the development of the priority standards.

## Power Standards

Larry Ainsworth uses the term "Power Standards" to describe those standards that are nonnegotiable in selecting the standards to be taught in a grade level (Ainsworth, 2003a). This was the starting point for the design of the Common Formative Assessments at Wayne County High School that would lead to the development of common assessments based on these priority standards. Teachers selected 8 to 12 overarching standards in their subject areas that exhibited the attributes of "endurance, leverage, and readiness for the next level of learning" (Ainsworth, 2003a). These standards were chosen based on the state framework document for the subject, state test blueprints, and college readiness skills denoted by many of the college entrance exam publishers. (These are the standards that all teachers in the grade-level course determined to be those that all students would have to master in order to satisfactorily complete the course.) This is not to say that these are the only standards that will be taught or covered, but these are the standards that all agree are the benchmark for successful completion of the course.

## "Unwrapping" the Standards

To be most effective, standards must be clearly defined. This process includes clearly articulating all of the knowledge and skills that a student needs to have mastered to be considered proficient on the standard. This is done by "unwrapping" the standards and clearly delineating the "Big Ideas" and "Essential Questions" that a student should understand and be able to answer if they truly have mastered the content (Ainsworth, 2003b). These learning goals would be clearly articulated to students and parents in the form of a syllabus that would be given to all students in all courses so that they have a road map for their learning. This was the next sequential step for Wayne County High School. With the help of Dave Nagel from The Leadership and Learning Center, the standards were articulated into a usable format. These "unwrapped" standards serve as the blueprint for the formulation of common assessments at WCHS.

## Curriculum Maps

Once the standards had been selected and clearly defined, teachers then designed instructional units based on the standards. These units represented approximately three weeks of instruction. The curriculum maps provide a pacing for content and ensure that all teachers have a platform for discussing current instruction and learning. These lesson units served as the criteria for selection in the construction of Common Formative Assessments for all courses.

## HOW COMMON FORMATIVE ASSESSMENTS WERE CREATED

The first step in creating the Common Formative Assessments was selecting the standards for the instructional units. Once these standards had been selected by each teacher team in each course, items were then chosen to fit with what was to be assessed. The final phase of the process was to create scoring guides and results indicators to ensure that all teachers had a common definition of proficiency. It is necessary that all have the same high expectation of what students should gain and be able to transfer from the learning experience.

For each instructional unit, teachers collaboratively determined which standards were most important to be assessed. This was done through the process of selecting what WCHS calls Power Standards. These are standards that all teachers in that content area have said are the "must-haves" when a student leaves that grade level or course in that content area. These standards were selected by teachers in teams prioritizing the standards found in state frameworks, national standards documents, and the blueprints provided by the state for the state of Mississippi's end-of-course graduation exams.

Once the Power Standards were identified, each teacher team set about "un-wrapping" the various skills and conceptual knowledge contained in each. For these skills and concepts, teachers then design Common Formative Assessments containing both selected-response and constructed-response items. These formative assessments are then given to students before instruction begins to gauge current understanding, and after instruction has taken place to measure the growth of the students' knowledge of the standard.

## CHALLENGES SET IN

One of the earliest challenges that had to be overcome was to learn the distinction between a summative assessment and a formative assessment. All had heard that formative assessments were needed. But all lacked the knowledge and skill to make that happen. This was one of the most challenging parts of the process. Once it was understood that formative assessment was to be used to make real-time decisions about instruction before instruction began, during instruction, and even after instruction, the staff began to feel more comfortable with the process of formulating the assessments. It was necessary to define formative and summative assessment in the beginning. Many of the assessments that were in place were assumed to be formative but were not. The difference was that these assessments were not used to change what the teachers did to teach, or what the students needed to learn based on the baseline data received from the pre-assessment. It became apparent that formative assessment is assessment *for* learning, while summative assessment is assessment *of* learning.

## ACCOUNTABILITY

Another challenge that became apparent in this process was creating transparency of what went on in all classrooms where similar content was taught, since all classrooms would be responsible for providing their data on these Common Formative Assessments. This was certainly a paradigm shift for Wayne County High School. Teachers were used to being able to close their doors and teach without much concern about being in line with common expectations of content.

The amazing transformation here was that after a short while the culture was transformed from one of defending territory to one of working for the common good. Teachers began to realize that with the standards increasing in rigor and complexity, maybe it was a good thing to not feel that you were on a deserted island having to face these struggles on your own. This was a turning point in the process of instituting Common Formative Assessments. WCHS's mantra was, "Yes the standards are getting tougher, but we are all in this together." No one person is responsible for meeting all of the challenges on their own. With the new accountability for transparency came the overwhelming support of colleagues. No longer did a single teacher have to figure it all out on their own. They could tap into the wisdom of the group. Even those teachers who teach singleton classes are still part of a team in their related subject so they can get professional support. As the teachers of WCHS moved forward in the process of using Common Formative Assessments, they began to see their power in helping to shape professional practice.

# DATA TEAMS

To effectively drive this process, the use of Common Formative Assessment hinges on a weekly early release day for students on which teachers have 90 minutes of uninterrupted time for collaboration. These are called "Data Days." In these meetings, teachers develop syllabi based on the priority standards, develop Common Formative Assessments, and monitor the effectiveness of instruction by comparing the results from pre- and post-assessments to goals set in relation to pre-assessment data. These meetings are based on before-instruction data, during-instruction data, and after-instruction data (The Leadership and Learning Center, 2010).

Before-instruction data is based on the first administration of the pre-assessment developed by the Data Team. Once given, all teachers compile the results for their students on the assessment, and the team then follows a five-step process. The first step is charting and analyzing the data from the pre-assessment. This gives a true picture of where all students in that course are at the beginning of instruction. It may also help illuminate gaps in learning. The second step is then to list strengths and obstacles that are apparent in the data. Next, the Data Team will set priorities based on the analysis of the data. Goals will be stated in relation to taking on the higher-prioritized obstacles. These goals are the chalk line at the end of instruction to determine if the desired learning has occurred. The fourth step is to select high-yield instructional strategies to be used in the teaching of the standards based on the information provided in steps one through three. Finally, the fifth step is to determine the results indicators that will signal students have mastered the content and skills of the standards. Basically, teachers should answer the question, "What does proficiency look like?" Using the pre-assessment results, teachers are also able to identify students who are not likely to be proficient after instruction, and provide proactive intervention to help get these students the extra help they require (The Leadership and Learning Center, 2010).

Data Team meetings are held during instruction to view work samples and adjust goals as necessary. These during-instruction checks for understanding can also be considered formative assessment as teachers may use this data to adjust the focus of instruction. Again, the same basic five-step process is followed. The accountability in this process does not come simply from having administrators and lead teachers embedded in these Data Teams, but from the collective norms that all must be prepared to contribute their data and contribute to the charts and graphs that symbolize learning across the grade and course for all students. This is where "teacher leadership" begins (Reeves, 2008).

The final act of these meetings takes place at the after-instruction meeting in which teachers bring in the data from their post-assessment. This is actually where the teachers will see that learning has taken place. When teachers see that only 25 percent of students were proficient on pre-assessments but 85 percent were proficient at the end of instruction, they begin to understand the power that they have in the instructional process. There is also a summative assessment component in the process in that at the end of the three-week unit a summative unit test is given in all subjects. This provides the much-needed summative component in the evaluation of the success of the entire process. In a sense, the post-assessment is still a formative instrument in that teachers have time before the summative unit test for students to fill in any gaps in their learning.

All Data Teams turn in minutes from their weekly meetings, and these minutes serve as the "look-fors" on administrative walk-through observations. These walk-through observations serve as an opportunity for administrators to determine if the work of the Data Teams is being implemented effectively school-wide and in all classrooms. This process helps guarantee that all students have the opportunity to learn the same content in a common grade-level course regardless of what classroom they may be assigned to. Additionally, success of the Data Teams process is measured against success on state assessments and college entrance exams, as well as success of students entering other training programs, including the military.

## CHANGES APPARENT DUE TO COMMON FORMATIVE ASSESSMENTS

Without a doubt, the sentiment of WCHS teachers is echoed when it is said that using Common Formative Assessments brings schools into the practice of making data-driven decisions. All at Wayne County High School had "Aha" moments when the first graphs of pre-assessment versus post-assessment data were seen. One of the most poignant occurred when the advanced algebra scores were analyzed; on the pre-assessment, zero percent of students were proficient, while after instruction the percentage of proficient students had increased to 76 percent. A graph makes this a tremendous visual experience for teachers and students (see Exhibit 1.1). This is the point when teachers and students can actually see that learning has taken place. Teachers can see how vital the actions that they take in the classroom are with results like this.

Significant gains in state testing results were seen in the first year of using Common Formative Assessments. At this point, WCHS is poised to make even greater gains as the process continues. Even more important is the professional growth that was experienced. The use of the pre-assessments to determine which students are in need of proactive intervention before instruction even starts has put teachers on the

**EXHIBIT 1.1**    **Advanced Algebra Pre- and Post-Assessments**

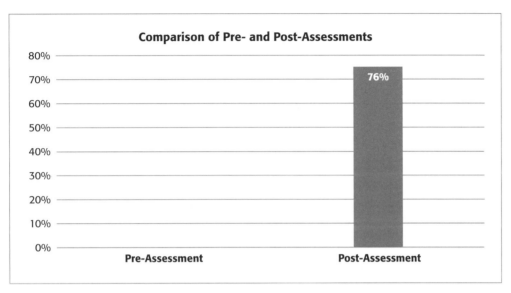

offensive when it comes to helping students learn valuable knowledge and skills. Post-assessment data provides the information needed for reteaching and retesting to give students multiple opportunities to show mastery. It is believed that Common Formative Assessments have made learning at WCHS more student centered. Professionally, the process has made the staff more likely to look inside for answers when students do not learn.

## REFLECTIONS AND THE FUTURE

In many ways, Common Formative Assessments have changed the way of thinking about educating students at Wayne County High School. The assessments provide the subject for conversation when discussions are held about students and their learning the knowledge, skills, and dispositions that they need to be successful in school. Many teachers realized they were not challenging students. When teachers gave their first pre-assessments, at least 75 percent or more of students were proficient. This provided the insight that teaching to the grade-level standard, in some cases, was not occurring, and teachers quickly realized there were gaps in student mastery. This was early in the process, and this was a powerful learning experience and turning point as WCHS moved forward.

As the staff at WCHS continues to refine the development of assessments and hone the knowledge pertaining to the insights drawn from both pre- and post-assessments, they look forward to being able to dig deeper into the instructional aspects of what assessments are telling them about student learning. The staff is seeking to draw closer connections between the instructional strategies chosen and the growth in students from pre- to post-assessment. Even deeper implementation of the Common Formative Assessment process is being sought by all teachers, for it is believed that without a doubt it holds infinite promise in helping to increase the effectiveness of educators and certainly increase student achievement.

I certainly would be remiss if I did not mention the overwhelming knowledge and support that has been provided to WCHS during this process by The Leadership and Learning Center. The associate from The Center embedded himself as a part of WCHS's staff and worked as a part of the staff from the first day of professional development. The materials that were provided with the Common Formative Assessment training have also proved invaluable. It would be hard to imagine the professional growth that was experienced taking place without the materials and the support. Wayne County High School certainly had the "will" to improve, but the professional development and support supplied by The Leadership and Learning Center illuminated the "way" to improve the school's professional practice.

## | | | | **GETTING REAL...** | | | |

As you reflect on Wayne County High School's real-time decisions, think about how their story applies to you in your current setting, and then answer the following questions:

1. Earlier in this chapter, B. R. Jones states: *"The difference was these assessments* [those already in place before formative assessments were instituted] *were not used to change what the teachers did to teach, or what the students needed to learn based on the baseline data received from the pre-assessment. It became apparent that formative assessment is assessment* for *learning, while summative assessment is assessment of learning."*

Where is your school or district currently at with integrating formative assessments within a more traditional end-of-unit district, state, or national summative assessment model? Where do you want to be?

_____

_____

_____

_____

2. *"Teachers began to realize that with the standards increasing in rigor and complexity, maybe it was a good thing to not feel that you were on a deserted island having to face these struggles on your own. This was a turning point in the process of instituting Common Formative Assessments. WCHS's mantra was, 'Yes the standards are getting tougher, but we are all in this together.' No one person is responsible for meeting all of the challenges on their own."*

Has this paradigm shift occurred within your setting? If so, what were the antecedents (causes) of this excellence? If not, what steps can you take right now to begin to foster this type of environment?

_____

_____

_____

_____

3. *"All Data Teams turn in minutes from their weekly meetings, and these minutes serve as the 'look-fors' on administrative walk-through observations. These walk-through observations serve as an opportunity for administrators to determine if the work of the Data Teams is being implemented effectively school-wide and in all classrooms."*

This level of accountability and monitoring on behalf of the school's administration set the stage for success in creating solid Common Formative Assessments. What examples of monitoring exist in your building? Is what your school values (current initiatives or areas of focus for educators) monitored?

_____

_____

_____

_____

4. One of the "Aha" moments enjoyed by advanced algebra teachers at Wayne County High School was the realization that the number of students proficient on an administered assessment rose from zero percent to 76 percent proficient (pre- to post-assessment).

   Building in small and large celebrations during the implementation of any new change or initiative is critical to its success and endurance. Are data-based celebrations a part of your regular routines? What can you do to further promote this practice within your setting?

   _____

   _____

   _____

   _____

5. This chapter describes the full process of creating and administering Common Formative Assessments. What were the steps WCHS took to ensure full-scale implementation from the beginning of the effort to the current state of this initiative? Feel free to create a flowchart or other type of diagram illustrating these important steps.

   _____

   _____

   _____

   _____

# CHAPTER TWO

# Spokane R-VII School District
## Spokane and Highlandville, Missouri

*"Until we identify what is most important and concentrate on those specific skills, very few students will become great. To me, the Common Formative Assessment process identifies those specific fundamental skills that give our students the firm foundation to continue to grow. It is the tool to monitor individual student progress."*

— Brent Depeé, Superintendent of Schools

*"What I see as the biggest value of the Common Formative Assessment process is that our building now has holistic accountability. We are more focused as a whole faculty and are pulling in the same direction to meet the goal of improving student achievement."*

—Daryl Bernskoetter, High School Principal

*"The CFA process has allowed our district to examine more closely what we teach, how we teach, and the level at which our students learn. It is a powerful tool for teachers to make informed decisions based on data during the instructional process."*

—Robyn Gordon, Director of Curriculum, Instruction, and Assessment

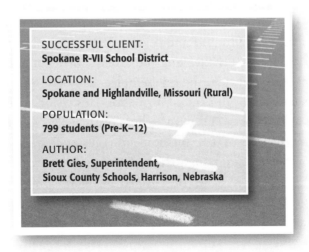

SUCCESSFUL CLIENT:
**Spokane R-VII School District**

LOCATION:
**Spokane and Highlandville, Missouri (Rural)**

POPULATION:
**799 students (Pre-K–12)**

AUTHOR:
**Brett Gies, Superintendent,**
**Sioux County Schools, Harrison, Nebraska**

# SCHOOL DISTRICT LOCATION, DEMOGRAPHICS, AND BACKGROUND

Spokane R-VII School District is located in Spokane, Missouri, in the southeast portion of the state. The school district is located approximately halfway between Branson and Springfield and south of Ozark. Spokane R-VII is an example of a small, already high-performing school district that wanted to be even better by taking student learning to the next higher level of performance.

The school district is composed of one Pre-K–5 elementary school, one middle school for grades 6 to 8, and one high school that houses grades 9 to 12. Since the district is small, the middle school and high school share teachers. The elementary school and central office are located in the town of Highlandville. The high school and middle school are located in the town of Spokane. The two towns are five miles apart. The school district is comprised mainly of nonminority middle-class families who have made Spokane their home. A strong partnership and support system exist between school and community.

The mission statement of Spokane R-VII reads that through a partnership, all students will become effective communicators, responsible citizens, and self-motivated learners. Staff members take this mission statement to heart. They are a very dedicated, collegial, and hardworking group of professionals who strive to perform at high levels in providing a quality education for all students.

Spokane has a strong rooted vision statement that emphasizes a partnership among staff, parents, students, and community with a resolution of four objectives vital to the educational success of all students. These objectives are academics, dedication, character, and communication. All adults in the lives of the students strive to reach these goals. The vision, incorporated into the district's Continuous School Improvement Plan, drives important decisions made in Spokane R-VII schools.

The emphasis on academics is a very important aspect of schooling in this district. Within the domain of academics, the district's vision statement stresses that students and teachers will promote and develop lifelong learning, maintain high expectations by presenting a challenging and diverse curriculum, provide resources to effectively maximize learning, and set exemplary standards through data-driven decisions and assessment of student performance. This vision statement is a driving force in the day-to-day operations of the school district. This school district talks the talk and walks the walk of their mission and vision statements.

As a result of the dedication to provide a high-quality education for all students, Spokane School District has earned the coveted Distinction in Performance Award from the Missouri Department of Education. This recognition highlights the academic achievements and progress made by the district during the 2009/10 school year. The district has received this award six out of the last eight years. To earn this distinction, the school district had to meet strict standards that are based on the Missouri Assessment Program test scores and other academic indicators.

Along with the district award, Spokane Middle School received the distinguished Gold Star award for being one of the six highest-performing and/or most improved schools in the state for 2010. To receive this award, the school had to demonstrate significant improvement on the state assessments over a three-year period.

Both of these awards are representative of the dedication and hard work of everyone in the school community, most importantly the commitment and dedication of the students in their academic journey. According to Spokane Superintendent Brent Depeé, "Members of the school district continue to work diligently to meet and exceed rising accountability standards each year. It is the joint effort of all the people within the school system and community that propels the district toward success in reaching the rigor in the rising standards and increased accountability."

## WHY COMMON FORMATIVE ASSESSMENTS

Spokane School District had been collecting data from several different assessments over the past few years. Teachers had been using benchmark assessment data to guide instruction on a broader spectrum but had not really used it effectively at the classroom instructional level. The administrative team felt there was a missing component. Teachers lacked classroom assessment data that provided timely feedback for instructional decision making. After much dialogue and investigation, the administrative team concluded formative assessment data to inform classroom instruction and learning would enhance the existing assessment program at Spokane schools.

The district administrative team felt that the information in *Common Formative Assessments: How to Connect Standards-Based Instruction and Assessment* by Larry Ainsworth and Donald Viegut (2006) encompassed everything they were already implementing, as well as provided the missing link of Common Formative Assessments (CFAs).

All the schools in Spokane had established Professional Learning Communities (PLCs), which provided the ideal framework for Common Formative Assessment work. The district was looking to utilize their PLC time to improve student achievement. The teachers and administrators were fairly well versed in looking at data, but, according to Robyn Gordon, Director of Curriculum, Instruction, and Assessment, "We knew we had to zero in our focus on classroom data to become more effective. As the accountability bar rises and the importance of closing the achievement gap weighs heavily on all educators, we knew we had to take the next step to continue to raise the bar of our current practices. We wanted to fine-tune our practices to make certain we are meeting the needs of every child in the Spokane R-VII School District to the best of our abilities."

The previous end-of-the-school-year teacher survey listed assessment training as one of the top needs in the district. This input, combined with a review of the current assessment practices, prompted the decision that Common Formative Assessments was the next logical step for the school district to embark upon.

Superintendent Brent Depeé, the school board, and administration felt that implementing Common Formative Assessments was the next logical step in their relentless pursuit to reach the next level of student achievement. Though he admits in hindsight they were not fully aware of all of the requirements to implement the CFA process, all district leaders, including the board of education, believed that this path was needed and their faculty was ready for the challenge.

## THE PLAN ON A PAGE

Just as a good carpenter has a well-defined set of blueprints before starting a construction project, every well-built organization begins with a well-defined plan, or "road map," to guide the organization through the process. Spokane developed a well-thought-out month-by-month plan that was clearly articulated to its administration and staff members on a regular basis. This guiding document was used to keep the organization focused and on track for the school year as the professional development for Common Formative Assessments was implemented. It served as a good reminder of what needed to be done and by whom with deadlines. The plan also outlined the key points that needed to be communicated to faculty.

The road map was a valuable tool that provided direction for the district in several ways. First, it connected all the powerful practices implemented within the district. The district was careful and deliberate in the development of the road map to ensure Common Formative Assessments were included as a key ingredient in connecting student achievement data from established assessments already in use by the school system. By connecting Common Formative Assessments with student data, teachers could easily see their value in enhancing teaching and learning of the established standards.

Second, the road map allowed administrators to stay the current course and to avoid implementing new initiatives. District leadership emphasized how CFAs were not a new program being brought to the district, but a way to better focus and fine-tune current practices.

This reassured staff that no new initiatives were being added to their already full plates for the ensuing year while they were learning about the Common Formative Assessment model. In fact, during the month of October, it was clearly articulated that one thing had to be weeded to prevent initiative overload.

Third, the road map provided teachers with opportunities to provide feedback. Throughout the year, teachers were given multiple opportunities to provide input to ensure the district was providing professional development that was timely and relevant. Teacher feedback was based on deliberate dialogue so teachers could be empowered with helping the district move forward with the implementation of Common Formative Assessments. This type of involvement is reflective of the culture Superintendent Brent Depeé and his administrative team have established in Spokane School District.

The road map was separated out on a month-to-month basis, August through May. For each month, six supporting categories were defined along with the corresponding actions that needed to occur during that month. The categories were: Goals, Professional Development, Accountability/Feedback, Assessment Administration, Professional Learning Communities, and Key Points to Communicate. Within each domain, objectives were identified that needed to be met within that month.

Two full days of professional development, one day in September and one day in October, were conducted to inform staff how to develop and use Common Formative Assessments in their classrooms. All staff members, no matter what they taught, were required to attend both days of training. All building principals, the curriculum director, and the superintendent actively participated in both days of professional development. The leadership team sat side by side and toe to toe with teachers to learn the process and to assist them in the creation of Common Formative Assessments. The high level of engagement by the administrators sent a powerful message to staff.

At the end of the first day of professional development, the leadership team and teachers collaboratively decided to set a goal of creating and administering one Common Formative Assessment in each classroom before leaving for Christmas vacation. This goal was established even before completing the second day of training. The commitment of the staff was encouraging as it reinforced their desire to fully utilize the new knowledge that was being invested in them. This was not going to be just another professional development day of sit-and-get and then go back to the classroom and do business as usual. This staff was committed to making a difference in the teaching, learning, and assessment process so all students could achieve at high levels.

Perhaps one of the most powerful design characteristics of the road map developed by Spokane is that it is a prime example of a well-conceived, yet simple plan, which could be easily articulated to any audience. And most importantly, it was not a complicated plan full of educational jargon. The details of the plan fit on one page (Exhibit 2.1).

## PROFESSIONAL DEVELOPMENT PRECURSOR

Prior to the delivery of the Common Formative Assessment seminar, all certificated staff members were required to participate in a book study. The book study was centered on *Common Formative Assessments,* and was conducted at each building with the principals as active participants. The central office team composed of the superintendent, special education director, and curriculum director also participated.

The book study was a powerful practice that allowed participants to have a leg up before the first day of professional development began. Teachers were asked to participate in two days of training to learn the Common Formative Assessment process. The two days were one month apart, but this did not create a problem due to the book study and the high level of dedication by the staff. Participants arrived with a common understanding and background knowledge of what Common Formative Assessments were and how they could benefit student learning. This degree of preparation allowed for deep and rich conversation between participants throughout the day.

Participants in the book study were given a detailed plan with requirements and due dates. Staff members were to read the first half of the book before the first day of training held in September. A week before the training, time was set aside in their Professional Learning Communities for a discussion that involved three guiding questions. Teachers were to discuss the reading and how it related to what they were already implementing. They were to communicate what help they might need. In addition, they were to identify five to six ways they could implement what they read in their classrooms.

The same process and guiding questions were used in their Professional Learning Communities for the second half of the book.

As a final requirement for the book study, staff members were asked to submit by the end of November a list of five or six ways for using Common Formative Assessment data to guide instruction. This provided for a direct connection between Common Formative Assessment data and effective teaching strategies. In addition to this requirement, teachers also had to submit in writing any area in which they felt they needed assistance. Teachers were also asked to provide any additional information they learned from their colleagues during their group meetings.

**EXHIBIT 2.1** Common Formative Assessment Implementation Calendar

| | August | September | October | November | December | January | February | March | April | May |
|---|---|---|---|---|---|---|---|---|---|---|
| **Goals** | Begin communications of district goals concerning CFAs | *Teachers and administrators gain background knowledge | *1 CFA aligned to priority standard *2 CFAs end of October *Weed 1 thing | *Use informal formative assessment in classrooms *Administer 1st CFA *"Unwrap" Priority Standard *Use data results from CFA | *Use informal formative assessment in classrooms *Administer 1st CFA *"Unwrap" Priority Standard *Use data results from CFA | *Use informal formative assess. in classrooms *Administer 2nd CFA *"Unwrap" Priority Standard *Use data results from CFA | *Use informal formative assess. in classrooms *Administer 2nd CFA *"Unwrap" Priority Standard *Use data results from CFA | *Use informal formative assess. in classrooms *Administer 3rd CFA *"Unwrap" Priority Standard *Use data results from CFA | *Use informal formative assess. in classrooms *Administer 3rd CFA *"Unwrap" Priority Standard *Use data results from CFA | All Power Standards set and "unwrapped" |
| **Professional Development** | Book Study | 24th – PD on CFAs Presented by Dr. Brett Gies | 25th – PD on CFAs Presented by Dr. Brett Gies | Discussions to determine how to best follow up with additional PD | Use teacher feedback to continue providing PD that is timely and relevant | Attend Powerful Learning Conference | Present information learned at PLC to all teachers | Use teacher feedback to continue providing PD that is timely and relevant | | PD Surveys to guide 2011/12 PD |
| **Accountability/ Feedback** | Teacher feedback from initial discussions about assessment | Review of survey results to determine further needs | What questions are you asking during walk throughs as a result of CFA PD? | How will you gather feedback from 1st administration of CFA? | How will you gather feedback from 1st administration of CFA? | How will you gather feedback from 2nd administration of CFA? | How will you gather feedback from 2nd administration of CFA? | How will you gather feedback from 3rd administration of CFA? | | Feedback from dialogue and PD Surveys |
| **Assessment Administration** | | NWEA- IBDs- Proficiency % - Instructional Changes- What data did you use? How did you use it? | NWEA- State Assessment- What specific instructional changes were made as a result of data? -Interventions for students below projected proficiency? | 1 CFA *What was determined from: -individual class data? -grade-level/ department data? *Instructional strategies changed as result of data | 1 CFA *What was determined from: -individual class data -grade-level/ department data *Instructional strategies changed as result of data | NWEA- -What data? -How did you use it? -# of students projected proficient? -Interventions for students below projected proficiency? | NWEA- What specific instructional changes were made as a result of data? -# of students projected proficient? -Interventions for students below projected proficiency? 1 CFA - *What was determined from: -individual class data? -grade-level/department data? *Instructional strategies changed as result | | MAP/EOC- What data? How did you use it? | NWEA- What data? How did you use it? |
| **PLCs** | Begin discussions of what data we already use and how we use it to improve achievement | -Group discussions of Book Study -Review curriculum map to review pacing | NWEA Data Review | Utilize time to create/determine Power Standards, create CFA, administer and review data | Utilize time to create/determine Power Standards, create CFA, administer and review data | Work on setting Power Standards and CFA | Work on setting Power Standards and CFA | Review Power Standards and align vertically | | Conclude work on Power Standards and alignment |
| **Key Points to Communicate** | Data usage, instructional pacing | -Importance of determining Power Standards -Listen to feedback from teachers! | -Answers to FAQ -What to bring October 25 | Continually reinforce that this is a marathon not a sprint. Keep open and consistent dialogue | Continually reinforce that this is a marathon not a sprint. Keep open and consistent dialogue | -Data usage to guide instructional practices -Instructional data/student data | -Data usage to guide instructional practices -Instructional data/student data | Continual dialogue concerning importance of the process and integrating | | Reflection of this year and how we can improve next year |

The purpose of the book study was twofold. First, it gave administrators a mechanism for holding teachers accountable for using resources purchased by the district. This was to avoid the situation where materials are purchased and distributed to teachers, but never used.

Second, it enabled teachers to build common background knowledge that ultimately enhanced their professional development experience. In the words of Robyn Gordon, "Our administrative team had a great deal of discussion on conducting a book study with the teachers. We decided it might be best to have the teachers read the Ainsworth [and Viegut] book prior to our CFA professional development. Every teacher is at a different level with their pedagogical experience and knowledge base, so we thought it might be beneficial to provide them the opportunity to gain some background knowledge about CFAs prior to the initial professional development day." The administrative team's decision to use a book study turned out to be a very worthwhile one.

Because of the book study, participants who attended the training were prepared to ask questions. They were motivated and eager to learn more and had a strong desire to apply the knowledge they had gained by reading the book. While the book study developed common knowledge, it more importantly provided for reflection about current practices and how Common Formative Assessments could be utilized in day-to-day instructional practices. Each teacher or teacher group turned in a reflection to their building principal, which provided great feedback to the principals and to the central office administrative team.

## INVOLVED LEADERSHIP AT EVERY LEVEL

When Spokane R-VII began this journey, the administrative team conducted an internal book study among themselves. Each week, the building principals along with the superintendent and curriculum director read a chapter of the book and discussed ways in which they believed Common Formative Assessments could best be implemented. The team wanted to infuse this process into their existing PLC model to work in conjunction with the current assessment practices. It was important to the district leadership team to implement the Common Formative Assessment process in a manner such that teachers would not perceive it as being just one more thing to do. The administrators thought this was vital to a successful implementation of Common Formative Assessments if they were to be used on a regular basis throughout the district. The leadership team had a strong desire to build upon the good things already in place in the district while not creating additional work for teachers.

After the district leadership team completed their book study, the decision was made to involve teachers in a book study. Since the principals had already participated in a book study, they became the leaders in this process with the teachers. Teachers were given the option to work in groups or individually, depending on what worked best for their teaching schedule. Principals were the first point of contact to gather feedback and information from teachers as they read through the book and had questions about the process that they were about to embark upon. This served as a good opportunity for the administrative team to gauge the teachers' feelings and perceptions of CFAs before going through the initial training. The curriculum director also participated in the group discussions.

All administrators were actively involved in the training sessions. During work time, principals spread out to work with their teachers, and the superintendent and curriculum director spent time working with teachers at all building levels. The administrative team felt it was important to work alongside teachers so they had a better perspective on appropriate time frames and expectations for implementation of the CFA process.

Superintendent Depeé believes that as the district leader, he cannot ask anyone to do something for the organization unless he is fully prepared to ask the same thing of himself. He serves as the front man on initiatives and holds himself fully accountable for the success or lack of success in the implementation of Common Formative Assessments. Superintendent Depeé set clear goals and expectations at the onset of implementing CFAs in his district. He remains committed to the process and involved in the monitoring of the progress being made.

Since completing the CFA training, building principals have worked with their teachers during PLC time to work on powering the standards and creating and administering CFAs. The leadership team has established a highly visible presence in the development and implementation of Common Formative Assessments in their respective buildings. They remain committed and supportive of the process as a means to increase student learning.

Since implementing the first CFA by the designated deadline, each building principal has been responsible for monitoring the process of implementing additional Common Formative Assessments, as well as keeping a pulse on the climate of the building. The involvement of the principals in this step was intentionally designed to ensure that the teachers were moving forward with the implementation. Once again, the involved leadership team set the tone for successful implementation and left nothing up to chance.

The leadership team is very good at keeping in touch with the teachers. One of the ways Robyn Gordon does this is through structured dialogue with teachers on a regular basis. She takes every opportunity possible to actively listen to teachers individually. This allows teachers to share their feelings, frustrations, successes, and revelations about using CFAs in the classroom. Robyn Gordon also sets time aside to listen to principals, much in the same manner as she does with teachers. She strives to be supportive in all aspects of the implementation process.

## KEY INGREDIENTS FOR SUCCESS

Spokane R-VII is a small district with a history of good student performance for the past several years. What sets this school district apart from many others is the strong desire to move from being a good school district to being a great school district. Its small size, which can be a real challenge at times, does not hinder its accomplishments. Implementing Common Formative Assessments requires a great deal of collaboration among staff. Spokane educators did not allow their district's size to present a roadblock to their desire to take student learning to the next level. Here are several key ingredients that led to the successful implementation of CFAs for Spokane:

- Active leadership involvement by the superintendent, curriculum director, special education director, and building principals at all stages of the implementation process
- The establishment of clear goals and the communication of expectations on a regular basis to the staff by the leadership team
- Monitoring the use of the process at all grade levels on a frequent basis by the building principals
- Opportunities for honest and open dialogue on a regular basis between staff and between district leaders before and during the implementation process
- A strong support system that empowered teachers and administrators during the learning process
- A culture of commitment, collaboration, and a strong desire to make the Common Formative Assessments an effective tool to improve student learning

Spokane Schools discovered that implementing a key district-wide initiative of this magnitude required constant and sometimes uncomfortable dialogue. The dialogue was necessary to keep everyone's focus and effort targeted on the goal of CFA implementation. By using a district-wide support system, Spokane R-VII educators and administrators have been able to sustain their efforts.

## | | | | **GETTING REAL...** | | | |

As you reflect on Spokane School District's real-time decisions, think about how their story applies to you in your current setting, and then answer the following questions:

1. *"The district's vision statement stresses that students and teachers will promote and develop lifelong learning, maintain high expectations by presenting a challenging and diverse curriculum, provide resources to effectively maximize learning, and set exemplary standards through data-driven decisions and assessment of student performance. This vision statement is a driving force in the day-to-day operations of the school district. This school district talks the talk and walks the walk of their mission and vision statements."*

   Is the mission and vision of your school or district the driving force behind the daily academic behaviors of teachers and students? Support your response with concrete examples.

   _____

   _____

   _____

   _____

2. *"We knew we had to zero in our focus on classroom data to become more effective. As the accountability bar rises and the importance of closing the achievement gap weighs heavily on all educators, we knew we had to take the next step to continue to raise the bar of our current practices. We wanted to fine-tune our practices to make certain we are meeting the needs of every child in the Spokane R-VII School District to the best of our abilities."*

   As you read this statement, circle the words that catch your attention. Why did they capture your interest?

   _____

   _____

   _____

   _____

3.  The following statement in the chapter is an example of the forward thinking that exists in Spokane Schools: *"At the end of the first day of professional development, the leadership team and teachers collaboratively decided to set a goal of creating and administering one Common Formative Assessment in each classroom before leaving for Christmas vacation. The goal was established even before completing the second day of training."*

    As you reflect upon the chapter, what other behaviors also demonstrate this way of pushing the envelope and maximizing opportunity?

    _____

    _____

    _____

    _____

4.  To prepare for professional development sessions on Common Formative Assessments, the faculty engaged in a book study on the topic in order to build a platform for learning to occur. Has your staff ever used this method to spark interest and ensure understanding at the beginning of implementing a new initiative? If not, what printed or electronic material could you introduce to help any new learning on formative assessment stick?

    _____

    _____

    _____

    _____

# CHAPTER THREE

# Bennie Dover Jackson Middle School and New London High School
## New London, Connecticut

*"The manner in which adults (administrators and teachers) view, approach, and engage in their work has been dramatically transformed. A staff that now uses data to drive instruction, and works together to achieve a common goal, has emerged. Rather than waiting until the end of the year to determine if there was credible evidence of student learning by using state high-stakes tests, students now demonstrate their understanding in a variety of formats through the use of formative assessments. Additionally, consistent expectations within grade levels, courses, and assessments have risen to the forefront, as well as common understanding of proficiency."*

—William Thompson, Principal

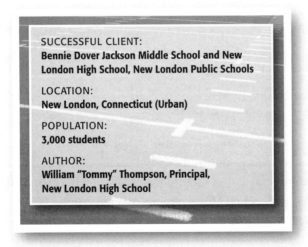

SUCCESSFUL CLIENT:
**Bennie Dover Jackson Middle School and New London High School, New London Public Schools**

LOCATION:
**New London, Connecticut (Urban)**

POPULATION:
**3,000 students**

AUTHOR:
**William "Tommy" Thompson, Principal, New London High School**

# New London's Story

## DEMOGRAPHICS AND BACKGROUND

New London Public School District is a small urban district with a big-city feel, and is comprised of approximately 3,000 students and 300 teachers. There are four elementary schools, a middle school, and a small magnet middle school and a high school, which are actually two schools in one. The student body is ethnically diverse, consisting of 46 percent Hispanic, 36 percent African American, and 17 percent Caucasian students. About 85 percent of the students qualify for free and/or reduced lunch, and 20 percent of the students speak Spanish. Research tells us many factors contribute to student achievement, but we know in New London, demographics will not determine our destiny! This story will focus on the evolution of our secondary schools and how a system-based approach provided the accountability required to move educators from theory to practice and consequently redefined how we do business.

Prior to the district working with The Center, at our best, we had islands of excellence and some "rock star" teachers. Additionally, we had a generally hardworking staff that had the ability to make connections with kids and manage classrooms. However, there was an absence of curricular and instructional focus. For example, two world history teachers who were in rooms adjacent to each other were teaching historical periods based on their individual partialities. Additionally, they had no common skill focus. This resulted in huge knowledge and skill gaps for the students who would leave, in theory, the same course. This example was not atypical of the conditions that existed in many schools in which I have been a teacher. As Rick DuFour has often said about staff throughout the country, we were "united by a common parking lot." In other words, the only thing we had in common was the lot in which we parked our cars, instead of critical commonalities such as curriculum, instruction, and assessment. With a nonexistent system to address curriculum and instruction, we were left with the following:

- **Curricular Chaos.** In many cases, there was outdated curriculum or literally no curriculum.

- **Lack of Collaboration.** At the middle school, teachers were provided a "common planning" period that allowed for discussion of team logistics and planning and discussion of students' academic performance and social-emotional well-being. However, this precious time often digressed to "gripe sessions" that were viewed as unproductive by administrators and many teachers.

- **Independent Contractors**. In the absence of a clear focus on curriculum, instruction, and assessment, it was a perfect opportunity for teachers to go rogue. Any direction a teacher wanted to take in regard to curriculum and instruction was permissible, despite the results their strategies were yielding. This led to gaps in student learning and a host of other issues.

- **Think-and-Feel Decision Making and "Data Don't Matta."** Data was rarely used to make decisions. Some teachers were even averse to using data, retorting, "Data don't matta." At the building level, when the state standardized test scores were released, a staff meeting was held to gloss over the results, but that was the extent of data analysis. Therefore, think-and-feel decision making reigned. Just as in the many staff meetings I attended as a teacher, those who may have been around the longest or spoke the loudest championed school improvement initiatives. Consequently, a "spray and pray improvement" model fueled by emotion and, at best, pedagogical fads existed for many years. Throw as much as you can against the wall—if it sticks, great; if not, keep spraying until it does!

- **These Kids…** Although we have a very diverse student population, our staff was certainly not reflective of our student body. Many teachers grew up in the suburbs and may have experienced limited interaction with poor minority students. For some, this reality led to some overt and cloaked assumptions about our students. These assumptions ranged from the knowledge and skills students arrived with, to work habits and work ethic. Parenthetically, I should note that some of the best teachers I have observed were also not reflective of our student body and held extremely high standards for themselves and their students. Whereas some teachers would deflect responsibility for student results, pointing to the community, the parents, the students, and whatever other societal issues influenced student learning, there were also those who would look in the mirror and ask themselves, "What could I do better next time?" when faced with a challenge.

- **Absence of Instructional Leadership.** Many of the administrators I have worked for or with have been building managers. As a dean of students, vice principal, and now principal, I can understand how during the course of a school day it would be easy for one to spend the bulk of one's time on noninstructional issues, from the irate parent to monitoring students in the café. This was the case prior to our encounter with The Center.

- **Absence of Accountability.** An unspoken agreement in the spirit of a laissez-faire approach to accountability was the norm for administrators, teachers, and students. For example, as long as teachers were teaching and the standards of behavior in the classroom were met, there was no problem. In my experience as a teacher in the district, there was little discussion about effective instruction and student performance in the schools. At best, some strategies were shared with staff at the occasional staff meeting, but there was no follow-up and no explicit expectation of the use of strategies in the classroom.

• **Lack of Efficacy.** Many well-intentioned and hardworking teachers do their best on a daily basis. What the media publicizes each year are the high-stakes standardized test results. Our district often scored lower than neighboring towns, which led the surrounding communities and people within our town to view New London as a failing school system. No one likes to be part of a losing team! Yet, annually we were told that we were failing despite our best efforts. Teachers really had no idea if what they were doing on a monthly, weekly, and even daily basis was working. There was no system to deliver feedback to students and teachers, which led to low morale. The only mechanism that existed was when the scores hit the papers and the community hit us! Let me tell you, it hurt.

## THE COMMON FORMATIVE ASSESSMENT INITIATIVE

In 2004, The Center began working with the state of Connecticut. Through the Connecticut Accountability for Learning Initiative (CALI), New London Schools was selected as a partner district because we were identified under state and federal accountability as not making AYP. As a result, New London was offered free high-quality professional development that far surpassed any professional learning opportunities that had been offered to date. My first experience with The Center was when our former superintendent, Christopher Clouet, assistant superintendent, Doreen Fuller, and our director of curriculum, Alison Ryan, encouraged teachers and administrators to attend professional development offered through CALI. In the spring of 2006, my wife, Ruby, and I decided to attend a Making Standards Work seminar offered in the district. For a couple with four boys under the age of 11, this was almost the equivalent of a date (I know, that's sad). The facilitator of the seminar was Larry Ainsworth, who I credit as the single most influential person to have inspired and influenced my professional learning. Larry has an infectious personality. He was able to demonstrate with conviction how powering standards, which is now referred to as "prioritizing" standards, would improve student performance. It made sense; prioritizing what would be taught in courses would help create the laser-like focus we were lacking. I left wondering how one would institute a curriculum that prioritized standards. How would this new approach be different from the curriculum that collected dust on the shelves for so many years? From my experience, I knew "sharing" best practices with staff and hoping they would implement them in the classroom was not enough. After all, I don't consider hope a strategy. Therefore, how could we turn this theory into practice and make it real for staff and students?

The answer to this question came in the form of Common Formative Assessments (CFAs). The idea of capturing what students know and are able to do based on priority standards, and then commonly analyzing the data in Data Teams to adjust instruction accordingly, would provide a system that completed the curriculum, instruction, and assessment loop.

In the spring of 2006, when I attended the CFA seminar, I came to realize that Common Formative Assessments are the lynchpin in instituting an integrated system. Common Formative Assessments measure student understanding of priority standards, create an opportunity for teachers to analyze student learning, and then to act on the data through the use of Effective Teaching Strategies. The creation and administration of CFAs would finally make our curriculum real. This would provide the impetus needed for teachers to take the curriculum off the shelves and design assessments based on the prioritized standards. In doing this, teachers would also need to create and analyze the assessment together! It was at the CFA seminar that I realized this system had the potential to provide the focus that was missing in New London.

As the vice principal of Bennie Dover Jackson Middle School, the day I returned to school from the CFA training, I approached our principal, Jaye Wilson, and proposed that we implement this powerful system. Jaye had the courage, confidence, and strength to approve the request. She empowered me to spearhead a reform that would eventually be replicated throughout the schools in the district. In an era when so many leaders tend to have a king-of-the-hill leadership style, where they push people down the hill who are trying to make it to the top, Jaye not only took my hand to help me up the hill, but once I got there, she elevated and supported me. As vice principal, I would assume the responsibility of being the chief architect of the initiative.

Now that the middle school had the green light to move forward, and had the framework from The Center, the next question that had to be answered was how to implement this initiative. Our leadership team brainstormed considerations that had to be addressed before implementation (I believe thorough planning and anticipation of challenges that would be faced during implementation led to our success).

We had to answer questions such as:

- How, when, and who would train staff?
- How would we provide the time for staff to get the job done?
- How would we support the process during implementation?
- How would we coordinate the system?
- How would teachers collaborate?
- Who would lead?
- How would we ensure fidelity to the process?

## Time

Time is our instructional currency in education, and how we spend it speaks volumes about our priorities! As a vice principal, one of my responsibilities, typical of the position, was creating the master schedule. Creating the infrastructure to support powerful practices is essential. It was determined that in our first year of implementation, one of the three meetings per week historically dedicated to common planning would be used strictly for Data Team purposes. By design, we were beginning to mandate how time would be utilized by teachers; it made sense to start small. We also would make a commitment to using staff meetings differently throughout the year. Items that could be communicated via e-mail were delivered in that manner, instead of using staff meetings, which allowed more time for teachers to collaborate. This same step was taken at the high school during my first year as principal. We were able to create a Data Team "duty" period for all core academic teachers who shared the same course. In order to do this, we had to decrease the number of teachers who could monitor hallways, the cafeteria, and so on. However, we were making a conscious decision to align our resources with our priorities. This approach to creating the time for teachers to get the job done at both the middle school and high school signaled to staff that leadership valued this process and would unconditionally support it. Additionally, the district commitment to the process was demonstrated when it was announced that two early release days would be scheduled per month to allow time for teacher collaboration and professional learning. The leadership had a complete understanding of the powerful practices, which was essential in order to create the infrastructure to support the process.

## Coordination

The administration developed an "Assessment Calendar" that delineated windows of time during which assessments would be administered. This was necessary because in order to use time effectively and efficiently, all of the teachers of the same course needed to be able to come to meetings with their data. After all, how do you hold a Data Team meeting in the absence of data? Sitting down with teachers and taking out the school district calendar to plot dates was an "Aha" experience for many. We didn't alter time, but teachers quickly realized how little time we had when creating this document. Therefore, this activity was critical because of the impact it had on instructional planning. We found this exercise extremely beneficial and I highly recommend it.

## Technology Supports Process

In addition to providing more time for collaboration and professional learning, resources were utilized to maximize efficiency. Software was purchased to aid in scoring and the development of reports in order to expedite analysis of assessments. Such reports provided individual student scores, as well as detailed item analyses that teachers could use to make instructional adjustments the next day.

Initially, in order to make the process easier for teachers, the administration assembled the data for analysis of student performance. This again demonstrated that the administration would support the process and valued teachers' time. We also wanted them to know we were willing to do whatever it took to support them. Eventually, as teachers became comfortable with the process, they assumed responsibility for it. At the high school, similar technology was purchased to support assessment analysis.

Additionally, Audience Response Systems were being piloted in classrooms. Students used handheld voting devices to enter their responses to questions their teachers posed as they checked for understanding. The percentage of students who provided the correct answer was immediately displayed on the board in a bar graph or pie chart.

Regardless of whether or not we were using this type of technology/analysis software, the bottom line was we were able to quickly assess students' needs and act in real time. We made a commitment in both the middle and high schools to provide feedback to students within 48 hours. Technology would help us keep our promise. By design, rooms at both schools that housed software systems were dedicated for Data Teams and were utilized to hold Data Team meetings that administration regularly attended. Posters on the walls in these rooms illustrated the five-step Data Teams process and served as a reminder of how meetings were to be implemented. The location of these rooms adjacent to the media center was also important so that our media specialist was available to help teachers with the technology and could act as the in-house guru for the software being utilized. This support was necessary for those who were not comfortable using technology.

## Professional Learning

Being conscious of information overload and deliberate in the "rollout" of the professional practices is extremely important. Our model of professional learning at both the middle school and the high school is product based. Prior to the advent of product-based professional learning, there was no accountability associated with professional growth. This change resulted in the positive pressure necessary to move our organization forward. Suddenly, professional development would become tangible because products aligned with action were required.

After the resources were secured to support the integrated system, a professional learning calendar was established. Over the course of three years, all staff would have basic training (in-house) facilitated by the administration and teacher leaders in the following order: Making Standards Work, Common Formative Assessments, Data Teams, and Effective Teaching Strategies.

Making Standards Work (MSW) training occurred during year one, which helped provide clarity for teachers and students regarding what should and should not be taught (after all, teachers couldn't teach every standard in one academic year). We began with MSW training because by prioritizing standards, we would know exactly which standards would be commonly assessed. A pacing guide was created for each course based on the curriculum. In cases where the curriculum was not written, we simply had teachers analyze the Connecticut State Standards and prioritize what students were to know and be able to do by the end of the year. We could not wait for the district to write a curriculum and proceeded with urgency. This is just one example of how we had to adapt and overcome challenges faced along our journey.

During year two, Common Formative Assessment and Data Teams trainings were implemented concurrently and before the student school year began. We implemented both practices because merely assessing students without a formal analysis and accompanying action would not impact student learning.

We realized professional learning is not an event, but a process. Just like students in a classroom, people arrive at understandings at different times, and support must be scaffolded to support them through the learning process. We knew that a couple days of professional development would not be sufficient for some. Therefore, e-mail reminders about the process were sent to staff along with "cheat sheets" on how to develop reports and run meetings. Administration, department heads, and teacher leaders regularly attended meetings and rolled up their sleeves with teachers, implementing practices together. Additionally, we often reminded teachers and administrators that it would not be perfect the first time. This was not a sprint, but a marathon!

## Monitoring the Process

Once all of this information began to flow, we quickly realized that we needed a system to organize the material. A no-cost approach was then developed using "public folders" in Microsoft Outlook, which allowed staff to access and send information from home or school. This was extremely useful for monitoring the process. I believe in the phrase, "Don't expect what you can't inspect," and this system allowed for inspection and support. The work of our community was now being captured, and it was clear that we were learning by doing. Additionally, the monitoring of adult behavior through the use of products being generated in teams provided a level of accountability that for so many years had been nonexistent. Now, all agendas, minutes, CFAs, pacing guides, and reports generated from assessments were sent by teachers to public folders and were reviewed by the administration and department heads.

## Teamwork

Development of Common Formative Assessments required teachers to work together as a team. Understand that teamwork is atypical. I observed more tears from adults working together in one year than I had in a decade in education. This experience reminds me of a reality television program on MTV first broadcast in 1992 titled *The Real World*. The show began with the narrator stating the following: "This is the true story ... of eight strangers ... picked to live in a house ... work together and have their lives taped ... to find out what happens ... when people stop being polite ... and start getting real ... *The Real World*."

Tasking teachers to create CFAs in teams resulted in things getting real! We were asking people who have traditionally worked in isolation to determine what content was going to be assessed, how it would be assessed, and when it would be assessed. Not only could teachers not shut their doors anymore and act as independent contractors, they would also need to work together and publicly display the student achievement results in their classroom and to their peers.

Initially, teams scoffed at the idea of establishing meeting norms for effective collaboration. These same teams would later revere the collective commitments they had made to run meetings, as they co-labored in creating assessments and at times experienced less-than-harmonious interaction. As a leader, I often wondered privately and in conversations with confidants where a "... good idea poorly implemented" and "learning by doing" intersect. Be warned, this system is powerful, and nothing worth having is easy. Anyone can steer the ship, but someone will need to chart and stay the course. Be prepared for the occasional hurt feelings and differing team dynamics.

## Leadership

Greater than building a system is the process of building and lifting up the people within the system. We can learn a lot from other leaders. As part of the administrators' professional development in our schools, we conducted several book studies on leadership. We held to the belief that we must be lead learners and continue to grow. We knew the minute we thought we had arrived would be the same minute we stopped growing and leading.

Leaders emerged from teams of teachers working together. The development of CFAs necessitated our schools move from positional authority to leadership. This was a change from the idea that one needed a title or to hold a position in order to lead. This new concept of leadership was at first accepted reluctantly, but soon teachers came to embrace this model and consequently had tremendous influence on adult behavior throughout the buildings. The work of Douglas B. Reeves, founder of The Leadership and Learning Center, supports the assertion that teachers learn from other teachers and are more likely to implement the learning they receive from colleagues than from any other form of professional development (Reeves, 2008). Leadership is the ability to influence, and it was the teachers in the case of New London who exerted the most influence on adult behavior.

## BENEFITS OF IMPLEMENTATION: FROM THESE KIDS TO OUR KIDS

Creating Common Formative Assessments had major implications for all students at Bennie Dover Jackson Middle School and New London High School. Teachers began to feel proud of student achievement, and we began to hear teachers refer to students as "our kids," "my class," "my students," as student performance was shared throughout the building. Whereas some schools profess they have high expectations for all students, they are not manifested in the classroom.

A situation that tested our resolve during this process was when some educators did not want to hold students receiving special education services and English Language Learners (ELLs) to the same standards. Consequently, they wanted to modify the "common" assessments developed by teams. Special education and English Language Learner instructors were major contributors to our teams when creating and analyzing assessments. However, despite the push-back, we remained emphatic in our belief that all children should be taught at grade-level standards.

The following open letter addressed to our staff at the conclusion of the 2008 academic year, and written by one of our ELL staff members, captures the success we had in terms of changing adult behavior and student performance. It also affirmed our decision to hold all students accountable to the same standards.

*Hello All,*

*As the school year winds down, I just wanted to share with you my thoughts on the initiatives this year. Over the past few weeks, I have been in the final stages of correcting student writing, including everything from the summative exam to work for their writing prompts. I am amazed, truly amazed, at what our students have been able to accomplish this year in writing. The growth that I've seen in my ESL II class makes me so proud, especially when I think back to last year, when many students first arrived to the country. Not only have they had to overcome the difficulties of starting in a new school, making new friends, and adjusting to middle school, they have had to learn a very challenging curriculum in a language that is unfamiliar to them. They are now writing five paragraph essays in their second language. There may be a few grammatical errors here and there, but their organization and elaboration is impressive. I attest this to the work we have done on Data Teams and with writing portfolios.*

*We've raised the bar and our students are rising to the challenge. Today, on a Friday, my students are finishing up the summative exam. The room is silent. There are a few children who are looking in the dictionary and writing their responses with fervor. When a student drifts off, the students in his or her group tap the desk as if to say, "Get back on track." They truly want to do their best. I am sitting here, sitting back and observing. They don't need me anymore and I am glad. They are motivated. There is no reward, only the knowledge that this exam somehow reflects all that they have learned this year. I am proud. We have all worked so hard and the results show it.*

*Our work with The Center and Data Teams is where it all began. We not only raised the bar for our students but for ourselves. I cannot convey in words the benefits that I have received from meeting with a group of individuals who not only share a common goal, but have had experience working and re-working the curriculum. Sharing strategies, hashing out a pacing guide, and evaluating the data, all changed the way I taught. Having the opportunity to glance at what the other teachers were doing gave me the insight that I needed to step it up a notch. Essentially being in my Data Team made me a better teacher, which in turn makes our students better students.*

*Boy, did I panic when the writing portfolios were introduced! I thought, "How on earth am I going to get my ESL students through this process?" Now, in the final weeks of school, my students and I review the contents of their writing folders and realize just how far they've come. One student explains that he chose to rewrite this paper because, "Oh my God, Miss, I wrote like THAT? I have to fix this; it doesn't even have a lead." The fact that writing has been reinforced in every subject area, that every student in the building has a writing portfolio, and that they know it will be in their permanent file, forces them to take it seriously and to understand the importance.*

*I am very proud of the accomplishments of our students this year. They have grown leaps and bounds. I know that they have acquired much more knowledge about writing and literary terms and CMT-like test answers than they did last year when I was my own little island. Data Teams, writing portfolios and holding high expectations have really made an impact on my students this year. I can't wait to not only see the CMT test results, but also to see how much better their writing will be next year when they can expand their writing and incorporate individual style. It's been a busy year, a challenging year, and in all the rush and occasional discouragement I don't want us to forget how far we've come.*

*Thank you,*

*Nickie Padilla*
*ESL Teacher*
*Bennie Dover Jackson Middle School*
*New London, CT*

Nickie Padilla continues to challenge students at BDJMS and is a perfect example of how formative assessments are changing lives in the New London Public Schools.

## ASSESSMENT LITERACY

Creating a system that incorporated Common Formative Assessments also resulted in common assessment literacy. Teachers spoke the same language and understood the differences between formative and summative assessment. Additionally, teachers learned of the benefits of various assessment items as well as how to develop scoring guides to commonly assess student performance. Students benefited from this common language as well. A teacher at the high school told me that when she started to explain the purpose of a pre-assessment to her ninth-grade class, in chorus they finished her sentence. Students having experienced this system were transferring their knowledge from the middle school to high school. Adult learning was having a direct impact on students' understanding of assessment rationale. Conversations about Data Teams, CFAs, high-yield instructional strategies, and student performance that were at one time missing became the norm.

## CHANGE IN SCHOOL CULTURE

While there has been improvement in Connecticut Mastery Test results following the implementation of CFAs, the adult behaviors necessary to sustain long-term outcomes have gained considerable traction. The manner in which adults (administrators and teachers) view, approach, and engage in their work has been dramatically transformed. A staff that now uses data to drive instruction, and works together to achieve a common goal, has emerged. Rather than waiting until the end of the year to determine if there was credible evidence of student learning by using state high-stakes tests, students now demonstrate their understanding in a variety of formats through the use of formative assessments. Additionally, consistent expectations within grade levels, courses, and assessments have risen to the forefront, as well as common understanding of proficiency.

## IMPLEMENTATION THEMES

There is no doubt that The Leadership and Learning Center's practices have the potential to change the educational landscape internationally. The framework espoused by The Center is based on sound educational research and theory. How to implement depends on many factors within your school and district. Implementing an integrated system in two different contexts, as a vice principal in the middle school and now a principal at the high school, has provided its own set of unique challenges. However, the following are some common themes experienced in both settings:

- **It makes sense, but it's a lot of hard work!** Teachers recognize that Common Formative Assessments and the process that encompasses their development and analysis makes sense. Many teachers have told me that we are finally "doing something" that relates directly to the work we do in our classrooms but in a formalized and systematic manner. One teacher remarked recently, almost in tears, "Tommy, this is so much work, are you trying to make us leave?" I replied, "No, I know this is hard and never claimed it would be easy, but how can we help?"

- **Building capacity.** An integrated system developed to scale in either a middle school or high school requires leadership development. Knowing that one person cannot manage and support this complex system, you must rely on key people to help get the job done. Developing those around you is the true testament of leadership. A leader's ability to build a team to carry out the mission will either propel or stall a change initiative.

- **Know where to place your focus and where to use the skills of other members of the staff.** At the middle school, we had a new department head who was still learning and coincidentally had to lead some challenging teams and personalities. In order to support this person, we brought in the literacy coach, Margaret Bucaram, to assist in facilitating Data Teams and supporting teachers. Under her leadership, not only did the department head benefit, but so did the teachers and students. The teams ended up becoming some of the highest performing in the school! Supporting leaders and knowing where to double up and provide additional support and guidance is critical to effectively managing an integrated system.

- **Loose and tight.** Coordinating and establishing dates and parameters within which teachers are to work are essential to operational success. However, it is also equally important to know that there are many variables that may influence one's ability to meet deadlines. Recognizing this fact and creating room for a margin of error goes a long way toward achieving widespread acceptance for assessment calendars. For example, by creating a 2- to 3-day window within which teachers are to administer assessments, rather than scheduling assessments on one particular day, is an example of being both loose and tight.

- **Celebrate wins and stay positive.** Find ways to communicate the truth that "Things are getting better!" and celebrate success early and often. Nothing improves morale more than knowing that what we are doing is making a difference in the learning of our students. I can remember some staff members who were initially the most reluctant and opposed to creating Common Formative Assessments parading their students' posttest results around the building. Efficacy, the notion that one has influence, was realized on a large scale as a result of CFAs. There are many other things to celebrate beyond student achievement. For example, we bought a cake to be presented at a staff meeting that said, "Congratulations NLHS Staff for creating 100% Common Assessments." This celebration recognized achieving a milestone as it related to our process. It cannot be underscored enough, that recognizing staff for their efforts is paramount. On a smaller scale, I never realized the power of a note to a staff member until I stumbled upon my wife's collection of "Thank You" notes that administrators had written her over more than a decade in which she had taught in various schools. They were keepsakes and very special to her. I was again reminded when I walked into our director of guidance's office and saw a note that I had written her proudly displayed on her bulletin board. In summary, recognizing effort on a school-wide scale, even through short all-staff e-mails and notes to individuals, is extremely important.

In summary, whether at the middle or high school level, the "game changing" mechanism will be the people who implement the practices. Common Formative Assessments will take time to develop and refine. Monitoring and supporting the fidelity of the practice, and the cognitive "heavy lifting" associated with coaching and coordinating to scale, do not happen overnight. Nevertheless, **this is the right thing to do**. The student achievement gains may not be fast enough for any of us, but these long-term and sustainable practices will pay dividends and can be implemented today!

## | | | | **GETTING REAL...** | | | |

As you reflect on New London's real-time decisions, think about how their story applies to you in your current setting, and then answer the following questions:

1. Principal Thompson indicates the following about his staff of yore: *"...we were 'united by a common parking lot.'" In other words, the only thing we had in common was the lot in which we parked our cars, instead of critical commonalities such as curriculum, instruction, and assessment."*

   Is your building or district united by a common goal that leads to common curriculum, instruction, and assessment? Provide evidence to support your answer.

   _____

   _____

   _____

   _____

2. *"We realized professional learning is not an event, but a process. Just like students in a classroom, people arrive at understandings at different times and support must be scaffolded to support people through the learning process.... This was not a sprint, but a marathon!"*

   Is professional development in your setting also viewed through this same lens? Why or why not?

   _____

   _____

   _____

   _____

3. *"Teachers really had no idea if what they were doing on a monthly, weekly, and even daily basis was working. There was no system to deliver feedback to students and teachers, which led to low morale. The only mechanism that existed was when the scores hit the papers and the community hit us! Let me tell you, it hurt."*

a. How did the implementation of Common Formative Assessments in New London address this issue?

_____

_____

_____

_____

b. On a scale of one to ten, ten being in strongest agreement, how would you rank your response to the following statement?: Our teachers know without a shadow of a doubt that what they do on a daily basis is working. Explain your rating.

_____

_____

_____

_____

4. *"As a leader, I often wondered privately and in conversations with confidants where a '…good idea poorly implemented' and 'learning by doing' intersect. Be warned, this system is powerful and nothing worth having is easy. Anyone can steer the ship, but someone will need to chart and stay the course."*

This statement highlights that implementation of Common Formative Assessments is a process, and not a silver bullet. What is your building's or district's approach to selecting and implementing new initiatives? Would you say in general you are seeking "the silver bullet" or you are working diligently to champion empowering processes? Explain.

_____

_____

_____

_____

# CHAPTER FOUR

# Austin Parkway Elementary School
## Sugar Land, Texas

*"As a teacher, meeting within Data Teams and administering Common Formative Assessments has significantly changed the way I plan and teach my lessons. I realized how effectively I could use my instructional time by analyzing data taken from the pretest. I was able to see what my students' greatest needs were, and what they were already proficient in. This allowed me to plan and organize my time and to maximize the time I have with my students and ensure proficiency. I was able to determine which students, objectives, or concepts I needed to concentrate my instructional time on."*

—Stephanie Deroam, Educator

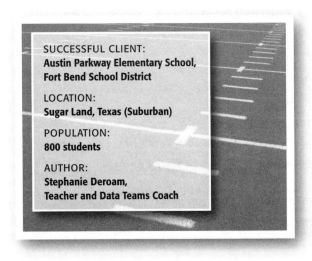

SUCCESSFUL CLIENT:
**Austin Parkway Elementary School, Fort Bend School District**

LOCATION:
**Sugar Land, Texas (Suburban)**

POPULATION:
**800 students**

AUTHOR:
**Stephanie Deroam, Teacher and Data Teams Coach**

## DEMOGRAPHICS AND BACKGROUND

Austin Parkway Elementary School (APE) is located in Sugar Land, Texas, a suburb southwest of Houston. Austin Parkway is a diverse campus with a student population of 803 students. The student population includes 7 American Indians, 353 Asians/Pacific Islanders, 83 African Americans, 65 Hispanics, and 265 Caucasian students.

Located in the South East region of Texas, Fort Bend Independent School District (FBISD) is the seventh largest school district in Texas and is made up of 73 campuses. Fort Bend Independent School District is the largest employer in Fort Bend County with approximately 8,500 full-time and 600 part-time employees, and 1,300 substitutes. Fort Bend is a diverse district with 31.36 percent African Americans, 22.38 percent Caucasians, 24.07 percent Hispanics, 21.99 percent Asians/Pacific Islanders, and 0.20 percent American Indians.

In 2008/09, FBISD was rated as an Acceptable school district by the Texas Education Agency (TEA), and in 2009/10 it earned the rating of Recognized. Fort Bend continues to show gains and growth from year to year, and it is making great strides in closing the educational gaps. The school district fully implemented Data Teams in 2008/09. Exhibit 4.1 is the district's math and reading data taken from the past five years based on the Texas Assessment of Knowledge and Skills (TAKS) test.

 **EXHIBIT 4.1    FBISD Math and Reading TAKS Scores, 2006–2010**

| FBISD Math TAKS Data | 2006 | 2007 | 2008 | 2009 | 2010 |
|---|---|---|---|---|---|
| All students who met standard | 77% | 79% | 83% | 85% | 87% |
| African American | 61% | 64% | 70% | 74% | 78% |
| Hispanic | 67% | 69% | 75% | 78% | 81% |
| Caucasian | 91% | 91% | 94% | 95% | 95% |
| Economically Disadvantaged | 63% | 66% | 71% | 75% | 78% |

| FBISD Reading TAKS Data | 2006 | 2007 | 2008 | 2009 | 2010 |
|---|---|---|---|---|---|
| All students who met standard | 90% | 91% | 93% | 94% | 93% |
| African American | 85% | 86% | 89% | 91% | 91% |
| Hispanic | 84% | 85% | 88% | 89% | 89% |
| Caucasian | 97% | 97% | 98% | 98% | 98% |
| Economically Disadvantaged | 81% | 83% | 86% | 88% | 88% |

Austin Parkway parallels FBISD in continuing to show growth and working toward closing educational gaps. In 2006/07 we were rated an Academically Acceptable school, and in 2007/08 we received a Recognized rating before gaining the rating of Exemplary during the 2008/09 and 2009/10 school years by the Texas Education Agency.

When tracking our third graders from 2008 to 2010, the data show the gains and growth all students are making in math, including our African American subpopulation, which has been our campus' educational area of weakness. In 2008, 91 percent of third-grade students met the math standard. In 2009, the same group of students celebrated 97 percent meeting the math standard. By 2010, 96 percent mastered the standards, showing only a 1 percent decrease from the previous year.

Austin Parkway Elementary has also shown gains for the African American population. In 2008, 71 percent of this subpopulation met the standards for all tests, and by 2009, 73 percent met the standards for all tests, showing a 2 percent gain from the previous year. In 2010, we did see a 3 percent decrease in the African American subpopulation that met the standards for all tests. Exhibit 4.2 shows Austin Parkway's TAKS scores in reading and math from 2008 to 2010.

 **EXHIBIT 4.2** **Austin Parkway Math and Reading TAKS Scores, 2008–2010**

| Austin Parkway Elementary TAKS Scores Tracking same group of students from 3rd to 5th | 2008 | 2009 | 2010 |
|---|---|---|---|
| Math | 91% | 97% | 96% |
| Reading | 96% | 96% | 94% |
| | | | |
| Austin Parkway Elementary African American Subpop Tracking same group of students from 3rd to 5th | 2008 | 2009 | 2010 |
| All Tests | 71% | 73% | 70% |
| Math | 69% | 79% | 75% |
| Reading | 94% | 87% | 85% |
| | | | |
| Austin Parkway Commended Performance on TAKS Tracking same group of students from 3rd to 5th | 2008 | 2009 | 2010 |
| Math | 53% | 71% | 63% |
| Reading | 54% | 58% | 53% |

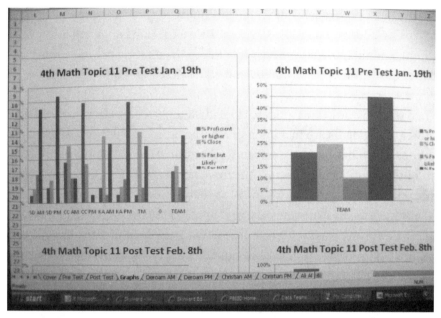

Data walls show Austin Parkway's fourth-grade math pre- and post-assessment results.

The campus data showed that our greatest area of need was in mathematics. The teachers decided to concentrate on math Data Teams in our year one implementation, while adding language arts in year two. Our campus goal was to increase the percentage of all students who meet the math standard, while increasing the percentage meeting standards in our African American and economically disadvantaged subpopulations. Not only did our campus want to show growth in our areas of greatest need, but we also wanted to raise the percentage of commended performance.

## IMPLEMENTING DATA TEAMS

I was chosen by my principal to attend the Data Teams three-day training provided by The Leadership and Learning Center over the summer of 2008, in order to become our trained campus Data Teams coach. In the fall, I led a one-day staff development session on Data Teams at my campus. I instructed the group on what Data Teams are, the benefits of Data Teams, and how to obtain and use data to drive their instructional decision making. We went over the five-step Data Teams meeting process, and the essential roles that teachers would assume.

Our campus decided to focus on Data Teams in mathematics during year one of implementation because, as the data pointed out, it was the area of greatest need. I met with both my principals, and together we chose teachers from each grade level to lead and guide their grade-level's Data Team. That same summer, I met with all the new Data Team leaders to go over the five-step process and model what a proficient Data Team meeting looks like. This was an excellent way to answer any questions or concerns that the Data Team leaders had, and was a vital step in the process.

The teachers and administration at Austin Parkway Elementary are the key ingredients to the success of Data Teams on our campus. They are dedicated and put in the time and effort to implement, self-reflect, and assist each other in creating Data Teams that will increase student achievement for all students and begin closing our educational gaps.

Scheduling was also important to the success and buy-in as Data Teams were implemented. In our first year, our campus set aside a day in the week that would be designated for Data Team meetings. During our second year of implementation, we had a six-day rotation where each Data Team had a 90-minute block of time, with the first 45 minutes used for Data Teams and the second 45 minutes used for team planning. This block of time was exceptionally effective because it allowed teams to plan immediately after discussing weaknesses and the instructional strategies needed to improve those areas of greatest need. It allowed teams to plan for differentiated instruction. In our third year of implementation, we kept our six-day rotation, but decided to use a 50-minute Data Team planning session in order to maximize instructional time in the classroom.

I will be honest; it was not easy when we first started. We hit a few bumps along the way, especially when it came to deciding what a good assessment looks like, how often we needed to meet, how frequently we should pre- and posttest using Common Formative Assessments, how to input data on the Excel template, and how to get through all the steps of the process in the given time frame. Many questions came up at our next Data Team leader meeting. We decided to contact another school's Data Teams coach (since this was a district-wide initiative) who was in year two of implementation as a sounding board to bounce questions and suggestions off of. We wanted to know what worked for their school and see if we could adjust and modify what they did to fit the needs of our campus. The best advice that was given to our campus was to just jump in and start the process; it was suggested that as we went through the five-step process at each meeting, it would get easier and allow us the opportunity to fine-tune and become more efficient and effective.

Our school utilized a common computer drive onto which the data for all grade levels was uploaded. This was helpful because I was able to have access to the Data Team charts for all grade levels. Periodically, I would check the charts to see if any grade level needed extra training or support. When a group ran into a glitch, my

An Austin Parkway Data Team meets to create formative assessments.

principal worked out a schedule to allow me to meet with that specific team. I was then able to clarify any confusion or answer any questions that they had on an individual team basis.

We also leveraged Data Teams on our campus as examples of proficient implementation to serve as models for other Data Teams who weren't quite meeting standard. We invited teams to sit in and observe meetings of other grade-level teams. This was a valuable approach and helped teachers observe what a good assessment looks like, how data was disaggregated and charted, how to write a SMART goal, how to identify strengths and weaknesses, how to select powerful instructional strategies, and how to plan differentiated lessons.

During our first year of implementation, we noticed different levels of rigor in our Common Formative Assessments. We decided we wanted to increase the rigor and consistency, so we chose to have all grade levels use the math assessments that were provided with our textbook, enVision, which is an incredibly useful resource for our math teachers. It is teacher friendly and correlates with our Texas Essential Knowledge Skills (TEKS). enVision is divided into 20 topics covering all six math objectives. Each topic comes with several documents that can be used for Common Formative Assessments. At the end of each topic, there are two end-of-topic assessments, labeled Form A and Form B. The similarities between the two assessments allow comparison and show students' growth from pre- to post-assessment. Each problem has a reference number that informs the teacher which lesson the specific problem came from.

We found these features of enVision made it extremely user friendly for teachers, students, and parents. Teachers are able to use the pretest data to see which lessons need more or less attention, while both students and parents are able to see which lesson to refer to in order to review or get extra practice. In addition to Form A and Form B assessments, there is a Free Response Assessment and a Performance Task Assessment to choose from, as well as benchmark assessments within each topic and an Exam View CD that allows teachers to create their own assessments.

Once teachers had access to good Common Formative Assessments, our next goal was to promote effective dialogue and discussions about the results of our pretests among the team members. Teachers shared the methods that work for them when charting data. It was our third-grade teacher, Mrs. Spearmen, who created the Excel chart our campus uses to help pinpoint the students' strengths and weaknesses. The chart lists each student's name so that the teachers can put an "X" next to the questions each child missed. The chart contains a formula that highlights all questions missed by seven or more students. The information from this chart is used to guide our discussions during each Data Team meeting. This document has been helpful in keeping the meeting focused, and the dialogue both informative and valuable. An example of an Excel spreadsheet used to chart student data is reproduced in Exhibit 4.3.

The reversed sections (white type on black) of the chart provide some insight into the needs of my classroom. I can see that the majority of my students struggled with questions 9, 12, 13, and 15, which are questions covered in lessons 3-1, 3-5, and 3-7. I am able to look at my pretest and see what was difficult about the particular questions the students missed. I am also empowered to ask whether it was the concept, wording, or vocabulary that caused the difficulty on the missed questions, or if the questions were not good ones and need to be looked at before giving the posttest. After these inquiries are made, the resulting information is discussed at our next Data Team meeting. The gray-highlighted sections of the chart indicate students who are not proficient. As a grade level, we determined a score of 75 percent or higher would classify a student as proficient.

During our second year of implementation, we decided to continue with math and add a language arts Data Team. Again, we chose our language arts teachers who were natural leaders to take on the role of leading the language arts Data Teams. We are now in our third year of implementation and continue to work on strengthening both of these content areas.

## Student Pretest Data

**EXHIBIT 4.3**

| Topic 3 Pre | 3-1 | 3-3 | 3-6 | 3-2 | 3-7 | 3-1 | 3-4 | 3-8 | 3-1 | 3-5 | 3-3 | 3-5 | 3-7 | 3-6 | 3-7 | | | |
|---|---|---|---|---|---|---|---|---|---|---|---|---|---|---|---|---|---|---|
| **Name/Question** | Question 1 | Question 2 | Question 3 | Question 4 | Question 5 | Question 6 | Question 7 | Question 8 | Question 9 | Question 10 | Question 11 | Question 12 | Question 13 | Question 14 | Question 15 | Student Incorrect | Correct | Percentage |
| Leena | | | | | | | x | | x | x | x | x | x | x | x | 8 | 7 | 46.7 |
| Lana | | | | x | | | | | | | | x | x | | x | 4 | 11 | 73.3 |
| Ali | | | | | | | | | | | | x | x | | | 2 | 13 | 86.7 |
| Caleb | | x | | | | | | | x | | x | x | x | | x | 6 | 9 | 60 |
| Jennifer | | | | | | | | | | | | x | x | | | 2 | 13 | 86.7 |
| Mark | | | | | | | | | | | | | | | | 0 | 15 | 100 |
| Evan | | | | | | | | | | | | | | | | 0 | 15 | 100 |
| Sidney | | | | x | x | | x | | x | | | x | x | | x | 7 | 8 | 53.3 |
| Savannah | | | | | | | | | x | | x | x | | | x | 4 | 11 | 73.3 |
| Sammy | | | | | x | | | | | | | | | | | 1 | 14 | 93.3 |
| Ariyon | | x | | | | | | | | x | x | | x | x | x | 6 | 9 | 60 |
| Noah | | | x | | | | | | | | | | | | x | 2 | 13 | 86.7 |
| Carole | | x | x | | | | | | | | | | | x | x | 4 | 11 | 73.3 |
| Callie | | | | | | | | | | | | | | | | 0 | 15 | 100 |
| Brendan | | | | | | | | | x | | | | | | x | 2 | 13 | 86.7 |
| Rithik | | | | | | | | | | | | | | | | 0 | 15 | 100 |
| BJ | | x | | | | | | | | x | x | | x | | x | 5 | 10 | 66.7 |
| Marina | | | | | | | | | | | | | x | | | 1 | 14 | 93.3 |
| Jacob | | | | | | | | | | | | x | x | | | 2 | 13 | 86.7 |
| Kolby | | | | | | | | | x | | x | x | | | | 3 | 12 | 80 |
| Lee | | | | x | | | | | x | | | | x | | x | 4 | 11 | 73.3 |
| Maria | | | | | | | | | | | | | | | | 0 | 15 | 100 |
| **Total Incorrect** | 0 | 0 | 4 | 4 | 3 | 0 | 2 | 0 | 7 | 3 | 6 | 9 | 11 | 3 | 11 | | | |

# THE VIEW FROM THREE YEARS OUT

As a teacher, meeting in Data Teams and administering Common Formative Assessments has significantly changed the way I plan and teach my lessons. I realized how effectively I could use my instructional time by analyzing data taken from the pretest. I was able to see what my students' greatest needs were, and what they were already proficient in. This allowed me to plan and organize my time and to maximize the time I have with my students and ensure proficiency. I was able to determine which students, objectives, or concepts I needed to concentrate my instructional time on, so I could work with students on concepts that they were still struggling with and increase rigor for the students who showed proficiency. Data Teams provide educators the data and necessary documentation regarding students who are consistently performing below proficiency. This helped with the planning of tutorials and our implementation of Response to Intervention (RTI).

Over time, I noticed a change in my colleagues as their thinking moved from doing something extra to doing something useful and beneficial as we implemented Data Teams and the corresponding Common Formative Assessments, which allow for collaboration, accountability, and keeping teachers on pace with the curriculum. Often, the data gathered from all teachers in a grade level was very similar. This gave us the opportunity to plan together and discuss more in depth how we were going to teach a specific concept given students' misconceptions or lack of knowledge. It also gave us the opportunity to consult with each other and allowed teachers who had great results on their posttest to share their ideas or strategies with teachers whose results may not have been as good.

Common Formative Assessments make all teachers accountable, including those in the grade levels that do not give a state-mandated assessment. I feel that they keep me on my toes because, let's face it, no one wants to have the lowest-performing class or the class with the least amount of growth. The data speaks for itself. I am forced to self-reflect and ask myself what I might have done better or differently. When we look within ourselves to improve our teaching, it allows the students the opportunity to reap all the benefits that come from increased teacher effectiveness.

My team and I are able to see the results and value of using pre- and post-assessments to drive our instruction and raise student achievement. Because of this, we challenge ourselves to pre- and post-assess every math topic. Our math textbook consists of 20 topics and provides a pre- and post-assessment for each topic, which allows us to chart close to 40 test results a year, and this does not include the data we chart for our district assessments. Exhibit 4.4 is an example of the fourth-grade teachers' calendar showing the schedule for pre- and post-assessments.

**EXHIBIT 4.4    FBISD Grade 4 Calendar**

| FBISD—Third 9 Weeks, 2010–2011 JANUARY | | | | |
|---|---|---|---|---|
| **Monday** | **Tuesday** | **Wednesday** | **Thursday** | **Friday** |
| **3**<br>Campus Staff Development<br>Student Holiday | **4**<br>Third Nine Weeks Begins<br>Teach Topic 10 Fractions<br>Give Topic 11 Pretest | **5** | **6**<br>Data Team Meeting<br>Go over Topic 11 Pretest and Topic 9 Posttest | **7** |
| **10** | **11** | **12**<br>Give Topic 10 Posttest<br>Teach Topic 11 Fractions Decimals | **13** | **14**<br>Data Team Meeting<br>Go over Topic 10 Posttest |
| **17**<br>Martin Luther King Day<br>No School | **18** | **19** | **20**<br>Give Topic 12 Pretest | **21** |
| **24** | **25**<br>Data Team Meeting<br>Go over Topic 12 Pretest | **26**<br>Give Topic 11 Posttest<br>Teach Topic 12 Patterns/ Expressions | **27** | **28**<br>Give Topic 13 Pretest |

I realized how using the data from the formative assessments had changed my colleagues when as a team we decided to not chart our pretest data because we had so much on our plates that week. When we met at our next Data Team meeting to discuss our posttest results, everyone was in agreement that we would not skip charting data from our pretest anymore. Our posttest scores were much lower, and teachers felt they went in teaching blindly, not knowing what the obstacles were so that they could address them effectively. I noticed I spent more time on a skill for which the kids had a good understanding, while rushing through a skill that they were struggling with. I was able to clearly see what I would have done differently if I had had my pretest data. That, by far, was the turning point for my team. We all knew what we were doing was important, but did not realize the magnitude of its effectiveness.

A big success I am proud of is our fourth-grade math Texas Assessment of Knowledge and Skills (TAKS) scores in 2009/10. We were in our second year of implementation, and it was the fourth-grade team's first year to chart and disaggregate data for each and every topic. We were so proud of how well the students performed on their TAKS test and how they continued to show growth. In 2008/09 our campus was in year one of implementation of Data Teams. Ninety-one percent of third graders passed the TAKS test, with 53 percent of the students being commended. This same group of students showed gains in our second year of implementation as fourth graders, with 97 percent passing the TAKS test and 71 percent scoring commended. The fourth-grade team was only two students short of having 100 percent passing! Not only did we raise the percentage of students passing, but we also increased the percentage of students commended. Frequent charting of our data allowed us the opportunity to differentiate instruction and reach all learners.

Using formative assessments frequently gives educators the data we need in order to guide our instruction. It gives us the opportunity to plan our small-group instruction to work with those students who are struggling, while also challenging those students who demonstrate proficiency. This increases the rigor for all students, which keeps them engaged for the long haul.

Data Teams, and frequent formative assessments, have not completely changed me as a teacher, but have opened my eyes to how to be a more effective and efficient educator and make a stronger impact on every range of learners. I am able to utilize my instructional time where it is needed most, focusing on what truly needs to be taught. I have learned to look and understand misconceptions/lack of knowledge and use this information to plan lessons and activities that will keep my students focused and provide the information needed in order to make sure they are proficient in the objective that I am teaching. I find myself delving deeper into the curriculum, rather than just skimming the surface.

My students, along with their parents, have become accustomed to the frequency of my assessments, and also utilize the pretests as a resource for extended learning. Both parents and students know what students are expected to learn, and parents know how they can help their child at home. My students light up when they are given back their pretests at the end of the unit to correct their mistakes, and they are pleasantly surprised at how the pretest is now much easier for them to complete. They even laugh at themselves and are in disbelief as they look at some of the questions that they got incorrect.

Going back and using the formative assessment as a resource is such a morale booster for kids; it builds their confidence in the classroom and opens up the lines of communication for me with my students. If students find they do not know how to solve a problem from their pretest, they immediately will come to me and ask for clarification or they will ask a peer for help. This is an excellent way to foster peer tutoring in the classroom.

Students in my room take pride in and responsibility for their learning. As long as I continue to self-reflect and refine my teaching to become an effective educator, I know my lessons will add value and engage my students, who in turn will acquire all the benefits and opportunities that come with enhanced knowledge.

## | | | | GETTING REAL... | | | |

As you reflect on Austin Parkway Elementary School's real-time decisions, think about how their story applies to you in your current setting, and then answer the following questions:

1. *"I will be honest; it was not easy when we first started. We hit a few bumps along the way, especially when it came to deciding what a good assessment looks like, how often we needed to meet, how frequently we should pre- and posttest using Common Formative Assessments, how to input data on the Excel template, and how to get through all the steps of the process in the given time frame."*

   To implement the Common Formative Assessment process well, it is critical to brainstorm, talk with all stakeholders, and plan in order to address any questions that could come up. Have you begun making inquiries like those above in your setting? If so, what are the answers? If not, how can you begin hosting this type of conversation?

   _____

   _____

   _____

   _____

2. *"The best advice that was given to our campus was to just jump in and start the process; it was suggested that as we went through the five-step process at each meeting, it would get easier and allow us the opportunity to fine-tune and become more efficient and effective."*

   Planning for effective implementation of any new initiative is important, as mentioned above in question one. However, there also comes a time when it is essential to just begin the process, and refine based on new learnings along the way. When it comes to trying something new, do you (your building or district) tend to err on the side of overplanning, or diving right in without enough forethought? Explain.

_____

_____

_____

_____

3. *"The fourth-grade team was only two students short of having 100 percent passing!"*

These results are absolutely incredible! What adult actions at Austin Parkway led to this successful outcome?

_____

_____

_____

_____

4. *"My students light up when they are given back their pretest at the end of the unit to correct their mistakes, and they are pleasantly surprised at how the pretest is now much easier for them to complete. They even laugh at themselves and are in disbelief as they look at some of the questions that they got incorrect."*

Are the students in your setting being given pre- and post-assessments for each Power Standard? If so, are your teachers giving them the opportunity to go back to their pretest before the posttest is administered and correct their errors by applying their new knowledge about the skill? If not, what is stopping you (or your building) from engaging in this type of process?

_____

_____

_____

_____

CHAPTER FIVE

# Macklin School
## Macklin, Saskatchewan, Canada

*"It is a belief that teachers and students, together, need to be accountable for a new type of education, an education where students are actively engaged and become a part of the journey from the beginning to the very end. This idea of going hand in hand in education with our students was the challenge that teachers at Macklin School faced as they began to transform their own practices."*

—Derrick Cameron, Principal

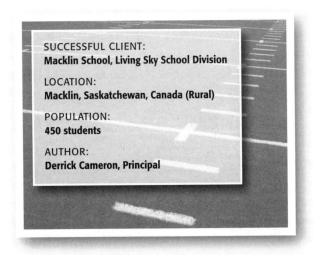

SUCCESSFUL CLIENT:
**Macklin School, Living Sky School Division**

LOCATION:
**Macklin, Saskatchewan, Canada (Rural)**

POPULATION:
**450 students**

AUTHOR:
**Derrick Cameron, Principal**

*"Growth means change and change involves risk, stepping from the known to the unknown"* (author unknown)

Imagine a school system where students and staff alike are encouraged to take risks regardless of the outcome. An idea where the goal is to become better at what we do, even if it takes multiple attempts. These are tough ideas to implement in a system where teachers are supposed to be the bearers of knowledge and wisdom and students are expected to demonstrate mastery on their very first attempt at a new task. The challenges these teachers face and continue to face are the same as those of educators across the globe. Teachers are no longer the experts because students need to master essential skills, rather than merely regurgitating the facts that a three-second Internet search will produce. It is a belief that teachers and students, together, need to be accountable for a new type of education, an education where students are actively engaged and become a part of the journey from the beginning to the very end. This idea of going hand in hand in education with our students was the challenge that teachers at Macklin School faced as they began to transform their own practices.

## LIVING SKY SCHOOL DIVISION AT A GLANCE

Living Sky School Division is situated in northwest central Saskatchewan. It encompasses a wide geographic area including the Battlefords, many communities, villages, First Nation communities, and Hutterite colonies. The division is located in the heart of wheat and oil country. The recreational and outdoor pursuits are plentiful, from camping, fishing, hunting, and water sports in the summer to downhill and cross-country skiing, snowmobiling, and ice fishing in the winter. The area offers a rich historical and cultural experience that is reminiscent of our past.

Currently, 31 schools are located in 20 communities. The schools include K–12, elementary, high schools, and alternative schools with a student population of 5,700 students. The diverse school population is reflected in a wide variety of programs that exist throughout the schools to meet the guidelines of the Saskatchewan Core Curriculum and local needs of the community.

## MACKLIN SCHOOL

Macklin School is a K–12 school with a student population that hovers around 450 students. The school has a full-time equivalent (FTE) of 28 professional staff members and an additional 16 support staff that includes custodians, secretaries, librarian, and educational assistants. Macklin School is located in the town of Macklin, Saskatchewan.

Macklin School, like all public schools in Saskatchewan, is required to use Saskatchewan Core Curriculum[1] in all areas of learning. Alternative and modified programs are also available at the school. The school also provides a very extensive arts education program with credits being offered in music/band, drama, and choir in the high school years, and music and band being taught in grades K through 8. Macklin School also provides the students of Macklin with a number of locally determined options including, but not limited to, religion or another option (K–9), calculus, psychology, and accounting. Students not only benefit from the academic experience at Macklin School, but they also are exposed to numerous clubs, school events, and community events.

## OLD PRACTICES IN A NEW ERA OF EDUCATION

Over five years ago, the staff and community of Macklin committed themselves whole-heartedly to a culture centered on "high levels of learning for ALL students." Macklin School was beginning to see an increasing acceptance of mediocrity in student performance and came to the realization that they were simply not providing an "A+" education for their students. The school had attempted to implement a zero policy for late assignments in hopes that this would act as a deterrent for students. What they found was an ever-increasing number of students who simply accepted the zero, as opposed to putting in the time and effort to complete the assignment.

Macklin School was not much different than a lot of schools in Saskatchewan. Staff believed their primary goal was to prepare students for postsecondary education or for the work world. There were numerous discussions around students needing to be accountable for their work and being able to meet deadlines. As a staff, numerous debates occurred about the importance of turning work in on time and what sort of consequence would be in place if the deadlines were not met. It was believed that meeting deadlines was an important aspect for students, and this debate was the focus of many meetings.

The assessment practices at Macklin School were very much like those that teachers had witnessed firsthand as they were going through the system as students. The students of Macklin School were given course outlines that identified certain grading practices; for example, daily work might be worth 10 percent of their term mark, and very rarely did they know exactly what was required of them to obtain credit in a certain course. Assignments were always summative in nature with stu-

---

[1] To learn more about Saskatchewan Core Curriculum or to view the curricula documents, please visit http://www.education.gov.sk.ca/curr-rsces.

dents only getting one chance at demonstrating their understanding even if they were to fail or to do poorly. It was not communicated to students how they would be graded or what an exemplary assignment might look like. The staff at Macklin School bought into the belief that assessment was almost like tricking students to gauge what they really had learned in the course. The assessments would be given to the students and the students would be responsible for determining what aspects of the assignment would actually be assessed. There was very little, if any, communication between students and teachers with regard to assessment.

Assessments at Macklin School, prior to 2006, were simply a tool to report a student's progress to parents, in-school administrators, and senior administrators. The discussion at numerous staff meetings would be around "how lazy kids were being" and "kids don't value education." Never once did the discussion relate to "What are we doing differently with our instructional practices?" Assessment was not used to improve classroom practices or to help students improve; it was always about collecting "a lot of grades" so we could report back to the parents how well their son or daughter was doing in class. Students were fine with these practices, because they were allowed to submit material that was not acceptable, and from time to time some would choose not to hand in certain assignments because it "was too much work." The teachers were fine with this as well because it was much simpler to assign a zero than to force students to complete the work. It was easier to give a low mark for poorly done work than to provide descriptive feedback and have the student redo it. These outdated practices had many people believing that Macklin School was truly preparing their students for life after high school.

## MACKLIN SCHOOL EMBRACES BEST PRACTICE

When Macklin began their journey toward a culture of "high levels of learning for ALL students" there was a lot of apprehension, as this idea was seen as another fad that would come and go. A Professional Learning Community (PLC) consisting of the two in-school administrators and a lead teacher then had the opportunity to attend a conference in Victoria, B.C., led by experts Richard and Rebecca DuFour and Robert Eaker. It was this conference that solidified the mission for the administrators, and they left with a very clear message that "teachers watch your actions and not your words." In other words, it would be the actions of school leaders, and not their words, that would sell staff members on this new culture. This was the beginning of one of the biggest challenges the administration team at Macklin has faced. How would they get a staff to "buy in" to all the advantages that a PLC culture would bring to their school and students? It became apparent that a key component in this culture, in order to move forward successfully, was the necessity to have staff members collaborating on a regular basis.

The team began the difficult task of aligning their actions with their words. Initially, they met with the director of education at that time, Ron Ford, to discuss the possibility of revising their school day. Once they had outlined the positive effects this would have on their school and students, they moved forward to discussing this option with the staff members. They felt the best way of having staff members get on board would be to provide time to meet in horizontal teams without it being viewed as another "add-on." The staff was overwhelmingly in favor!

Next, the staff and in-school administration team had its first meeting with the community to get feedback about having early dismissal every Wednesday and lengthening the school day for the other four days of the week. The support from the community was overwhelming too, as parents were ecstatic that the staff was making this strong commitment to student achievement.

The problem with this type of journey, however, is there are no clear guidelines on how to begin or what the ongoing process may look like. All that the staff knew was that they had to clearly identify the skills they wanted their students to master. While the conversations of the first few meetings were invaluable, the staff soon realized that they needed a framework that could better guide their weekly meetings.

Living Sky School Division booked all their in-school administrators to attend the Ahead of the Curve conference in Regina, Saskatchewan. There they were introduced to the work of Larry Ainsworth who outlined how a school could proceed with the PLC culture. Larry provided a clear framework for staff members to delve into curricula and get to the heart of what they really wanted students to learn. The greatest challenge the staff at Macklin School faced was finding a balance between teaching "content" and ensuring students "mastered" those skills deemed essential. Indispensable skills, or priority standards, were chosen based on the criteria outlined by Douglas B. Reeves. These skills were chosen based on the belief ALL essential skills had to meet the following criteria:

- Endurance

- Leverage

- Readiness for the next level (Reeves, 2002b)

The work of Larry Ainsworth and Douglas Reeves provided the staff with a framework to use in their weekly PLC meetings, and added a level of focus that was desperately needed within the PLC.

## COMMITMENT FROM STAFF, COMMUNITY, AND IN-SCHOOL ADMINISTRATION

As the staff of Macklin School began to address the idea of formative assessment, they quickly realized they would have to carry out a number of very difficult conversations. Issues like giving zeros for missing or late assignments, deducting marks for late assignments, and expecting students to demonstrate mastery the very first time became the topics of conversation in most of the meetings.

The struggles came largely at the middle and senior levels as these teachers firmly believed their job was to prepare students for the "real world." However, after returning from the Ahead of the Curve conference in Regina, where they had the opportunity to witness keynote speakers like Douglas Reeves, Thomas Guskey, and Larry Ainsworth, it became apparent they were operating under false pretenses. It was at this event that the educators' misconceptions were challenged with statements that contradicted the "real world" philosophy. Professionals in the "real world" are given second chances to improve or show improvement on a regular basis.

Douglas Reeves, in multiple settings, has discussed how professionals in numerous professions have multiple opportunities to demonstrate mastery, and that the current practices of public schools do not align with this philosophy. Most teachers believe they do what they are supposed to do: prepare students for the "real world" by taking a rigid stance on late and incomplete work. However, medical doctors practice their techniques on cadavers before they ever have the opportunity to utilize their learning on a live patient. They practice and practice until they display a certain degree of mastery, and yet schools expect students to demonstrate a high degree of mastery in a subject matter to which they have not been exposed on a *regular* basis.

As the staff at Macklin began examining these statements, they gave rise to even more challenging issues. What did the grades assigned to students really reflect? Was it best practice to assign zeros and "allow" students to opt out of work? Did students actually look at the feedback the teachers were providing? How could teachers encourage students to become more active participants in their education? These questions were beginning to be asked on a regular basis.

As rich as the dialogue was between staff members, they realized that there was a larger hurdle if they were to move forward with the concept of formative assessment. The community of Macklin was very supportive of their school, but they were members of the traditional school system that used the same assessment practices that were still being utilized in many classrooms in the 21st century. It was not a case of *convincing* parents that formative assessment was best practice, but more about *educating* parents, students, and community members that young people would be coached along the way (through the administration of formative assessments) to prepare them for the summative assessments that they were all used to.

Again, the dialogue between the various stakeholders was very valuable and challenging; educators were constantly being taken to task.

- "How was it fair if one student gets numerous attempts to demonstrate their mastery, and my son or daughter gets it the very first time?"
- "Students should not be getting multiple opportunities to demonstrate their learning!"
- "Why would anyone meet the deadlines if students were being given multiple attempts at mastering their work?"

These sentiments were being expressed by parents and community members fearful of new practices and skeptical about whether they would really improve student learning. As the parents and community members became educated on formative assessment, they began to realize their teachers were going to start utilizing the same practices that their athletic coaches had been utilizing for decades. Formative assessment, they realized, was not about inflating marks or pitting one student against another; it was meant to prepare students to demonstrate their learning compared to the outcomes that the ministry had identified as being important.

As much as the parents and community members struggled with formative assessment, it was equally as challenging for the students at Macklin School. They simply wanted to regurgitate facts on simple tests and choose not to hand in assignments that were challenging and time consuming. They wanted the zero.

As the staff at Macklin School examined this resistance from their students, the belief that the school had embraced a culture of mediocrity once again came to the forefront. Students needed to be challenged to "learn at high levels," and formative assessment would be the tool to help the staff implement this new culture. The staff not only acknowledged the power formative assessment had, or would have, on student learning, but they quickly realized this practice would allow them to make necessary changes to their own practices in a much more timely manner. Acknowledging this initiative impacted everyone in the building, and the staff set out to embrace a number of practices to aid in implementation of formative assessment.

## RESEARCH TO PRACTICE

Rick Stiggins (2004) argues, "Students can hit any *target* that they can see and that holds still for them." This argument became the primary focus of the staff at Macklin School as they began to implement formative assessment practices. A lot of the early work at Macklin was based on this idea, as well as the work of Canadian assessment expert Anne Davies.

The more the staff examined formative assessment, the more they realized it was utilized on a fairly regular basis outside the walls of the education system. According to Anne Davies, students need to know the starting point and where they are going to end up. It is up to the educators to provide guidance from the beginning to the end. Anne Davies uses the analogy of golfing. When golfers step on to a golf course they know where they are starting and they know where they are going. Along the way there are markers on the golf course that help the golfers with yardage, or they may have a yardage book (Davies, 2007). Needless to say, the staff at Macklin School agreed that they needed to be clearer with their students with regard to where they were going in their learning.

The staff also realized through their discussions that they needed to be clearer with students about expectations. The vast majority of the teaching staff agreed they needed to display clear learning targets for every lesson they taught. At first, the students were confused about why the staff was doing this, and very negative comments could be heard throughout the building from the senior years students. Students only wanted to be taught and were not concerned about the starting point or where they were going with their learning.

However, conversations in the weekly PLC meetings indicated that after only a week of implementation, students were quick to ask what their learning targets were before the lesson even began. Not only were they beginning to "buy in" to having a say in their education, but now they were holding their teachers accountable for best practices. The learning targets marked the beginning of formative assessment as the students began to agree they should have multiple attempts at demonstrating mastery.

Even though students were "buying in" to the concept of formative assessment, some of the teaching staff still struggled with the concept. Questions like "Why would students do exemplary work their first time when they get a chance or chances to make corrections?" or "How much extra work is this going to mean for me?" were still hurdles for some. A handful of staff members were going to fight formative assessment to the bitter end, because what it really did was separate exemplary teachers from average ones. For those staff members who embraced formative assessment and best practices, their classrooms were transformed into some of the most exciting learning opportunities a student could experience. Classrooms were full of students excited about learning and willing to do what they had to to meet the agreed-upon benchmarks.

Teachers began to implement a number of very powerful formative assessment practices. This began by utilizing a number of practices that would give teachers a quick snapshot of what their students had trouble with or struggled with before, during, or after a lesson. A casual observer could walk into almost any classroom and observe some of the most amazing "best practices" in current education. Teachers really struggled with some of the practices because they felt they were not getting an accurate depiction of what their students knew or were struggling with. Some attempted utilizing thumbs up, thumbs to the side, or thumbs down to gauge how students were progressing with the current lesson. Because teachers felt that students were looking at one another to determine how they would respond to a particular question, teachers began asking students to put their heads on their desks before asking questions. Students would then be randomly called on to explain why they chose the answer they did. This method of formative assessment allowed the teachers to quickly analyze how their teaching was meeting the needs of their students, but more importantly it gave them a tool to check for any misconceptions the students may have had and address them in a timely manner.

As the staff members moved forward in incorporating formative assessment practices in their classrooms, they struggled with determining if what they were doing was actually formative or summative in nature.

The enthusiasm the students displayed toward the newly accepted practices was difficult to explain. Students would look forward to the beginning-of-unit pre-assessments, so they could display to their teachers their prior knowledge, misconceptions, and areas of weakness. One of the superintendents, Brian Quinn, often spoke of how exciting it was to walk into classrooms at Macklin School and observe students engaged in their education through numerous formative assessment practices. It became very clear students wanted to be informed of how they were doing on a regular basis and they wanted a say in their own education. The elementary staff embraced the new initiative with open arms and experimented with formative assessments like exit and entrance cards, brain drains, KWL charts, and pre-assessment tests/quizzes.

In the high school, because formative assessment was viewed as a huge add-on, the educators needed to examine practices that would make sense to the high school teachers. They began to buy in to the work of Anne Davies.

The senior high English teacher, Kevin Burningham, and colleague Kelly Partington took on key roles as they led the way for all middle years and high school staff. The staff, including Kevin and Kelly, were very hesitant to begin student-centered self- and peer-assessment. The concerns centered on how to get students to objectively assess one another and get past the "This is my best friend so I need to give them a good mark" syndrome. Because of Kevin and Kelly's work and the leadership role they took on, a number of middle years and high school teachers began to co-construct criteria with their students. This laid the groundwork for students to begin self-assessing and peer-assessing their work in a very objective manner. The teachers discovered, based on the work of Anne Davies, they tripled the amount of feedback students received by utilizing self-assessment, peer-assessment, and the teacher assessment. This did not happen without setbacks and hurdles. Students had to be taught how to self-assess, how to assess their peers, and how to work collaboratively as a group to co-construct the criteria they would be assessed on.

Even though all staff members were using formative assessment, to varying degrees, the one criticism that constantly crept into conversations was the amount of time it took to provide descriptive feedback to students in a timely manner. As principal of the school, I had the opportunity to meet with Douglas Reeves in Vancouver, B.C., and during that meeting some of the challenges of formative assessment were discussed.

During the meeting, Doug spoke of a system he utilized when providing formative feedback. Following that conversation, I met with my staff to discuss the meeting I had with Doug, and I highlighted the need to take a more rigid stance with formative assessment.

Each student was required to submit a checklist with initials whenever they handed in a piece of work for assessing. If the classroom teacher came across a deficiency in the work, the teacher would stop their feedback and assessing at that point and return it to the student. The staff utilized this practice because of the time involved in carrying out formative assessment. Because the staff was encouraging students to focus and reflect more on the details of the co-constructed criteria, students were becoming more accountable for what they were handing in. As a result, students became much more conscious of the first drafts they were submitting to their teachers.

## CONCLUSION

Learning at Macklin School became extremely exciting and very rewarding. Students were becoming active participants in their education and were welcoming the opportunity to improve their work if it did not meet an agreed-upon benchmark. Many teachers acknowledged the fact that formative assessment was a tool meant to help them reflect on their practices and that the in-school administrators would support them regardless of the end result.

As excited as the majority of the staff, students, and parents were, the move to embrace formative assessment did not come without its critics. The in-school administration team would continue to challenge those staff members who continued to utilize outdated practices and were not meeting the needs of ALL students. Staff members were called on to answer difficult questions including, "How does letting a student sit and do nothing for over half a class meet their needs"? It was these teachers who were critical of anything that would be deemed "best practices" who had the most trouble transitioning to the new assessment practices.

The biggest challenge or disappointment the school faced was the lack of support from the director of education. The principal was challenged on a number of occasions regarding his school's performance. Why was Macklin School not significantly outperforming other schools in the division given the early dismissal every week to discuss how they could improve student learning? As the principal of the school, I would often inform senior administrators that formative assessment was not meant to increase test scores at rapid rates, but to help students bring meaning to their own learning and raise achievement over time.

W. Edwards Deming (1982) argued, "The majority of the problems we encounter in our work do not rest with the people who are trying to do the work, but instead with the system in which those people work." Formative assessments provided the opportunity for teachers at Macklin School to reexamine the current state of education as it related specifically to their students. While this was not the initial reason for implementing formative assessment, the new initiative required teachers and parents to reflect on their current realities.

Lisa Carter stated, "Learning is an incremental process, and it takes all of us working together to construct a strong, well-connected learning ladder for students to climb" (Carter, 2007). Because formative assessment had such an instrumental effect on the teachers' practices, they began to question some of the very foundations for which education was created. The teaching staff, along with parents, questioned whether "covering" the curriculum in the allotted time was in the best interest of their students, or if they should be utilizing formative assessment to truly meet the needs of ALL students in Macklin School. Not only did formative assessment become a critical part of the instructional practices in Macklin School, but the teachers also bought in to the premise that learning needed to be the constant and not time. As Lisa Carter stated,

> *When time is held as a constant, learning becomes a variable. If we are truly going to ensure that all students meet or exceed learning expectations, our school systems will have to be redesigned to make learning the constant, which means that time to learn will have to vary with the needs of each student.*

Formative assessments allowed the teachers and students to realize that learning was the focus of all education, and in order for that to truly happen, they needed to move at a pace that allowed ALL students to learn. Formative assessments changed the practices at Macklin School, and allowed it to become truly student centered.

## | | | | GETTING REAL... | | | |

As you reflect on Macklin School's real-time decisions, think about how their story applies to you in your current setting, and then answer the following questions:

1. The author uses the following phrases to discuss the assessment practices of old at Macklin:

   • *The assessment practices at Macklin School were very much like those that teachers had witnessed firsthand as they were going through the system as students.*

   • *Assignments were always summative in nature with students only getting one chance at demonstrating their understanding, even if they were to fail or to do poorly. It was not communicated to students how they would be graded or what an exemplary assignment might look like. The staff at Macklin School bought into the belief that assessment was almost like tricking students to gauge what they really had learned in the course.*

   • *Assessments at Macklin School, prior to 2006, were simply a tool to report a student's progress to parents, in-school administrators, and senior administrators.*

   a. Scoring guides complement effective Common Formative Assessments, as they allow the student and the scorer to have a clear-cut definition of success. Are scoring guides used in conjunction with formative assessments systematically in your setting?

   b. What do assessments mean to you and the educators surrounding you?

   _____

   _____

   _____

   _____

2. *"The discussion at numerous staff meetings would be around 'how lazy kids were being' and 'kids don't value education.' Never once did the discussion relate to 'What are we doing differently with our instructional practices?'"*

   In your setting, are educators focused more on blaming students, or refining their instructional practices?

   _____

   _____

   _____

   _____

3. *"…it was much simpler to assign a zero than to force students to complete the work."*

   This chapter tells the story of a faculty who changed their outlook on administering and scoring assessments. What is your story?

   _____

   _____

   _____

   _____

4. *"…teachers watch your actions and not your words."*

   Are you modeling the change you desire to see in your setting?

   _____

   _____

   _____

   _____

CHAPTER SIX

# Lew Wallace Elementary School
## Albuquerque, New Mexico

*"Teachers must endure the constant question posed to them by the students in their class: 'When are we going to work on our PAs?' If it were up to them, Performance Assessments would be what they would do all day, every day. Teachers have themselves commented, 'I wish I could teach this way all the time.' The defining characteristics of Performance Assessments are high student engagement, immediate feedback, and a diagnostic tool for teachers as well as students, opportunities for writing that matters, as well as multiple opportunities for success. In addition, they cover a multitude of skills and standards. They have it all.... What I am certain about is this. Performance Assessments have and will continue to endure the test of time. Budget cuts may come, and they have.... Nevertheless, Performance Assessments continue to flourish at our school."*

—Jo Peters, Principal

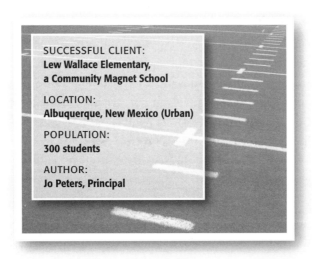

SUCCESSFUL CLIENT:
**Lew Wallace Elementary,**
**a Community Magnet School**

LOCATION:
**Albuquerque, New Mexico (Urban)**

POPULATION:
**300 students**

AUTHOR:
**Jo Peters, Principal**

# A Journey Into Standards-Based Instruction and Assessment

## BACKGROUND

Our school has an interesting history. Built in 1892, Lew Wallace was one of four schools within the Albuquerque city limits. Originally named Fourth Ward School, it housed 500 students and 13 teachers. The school burned to the ground on April 25, 1932. A new building was erected on the original site and reopened in September 1935. It was renamed Lew Wallace after a New Mexico territorial governor and author of *Ben Hur*. The school was declared a Historic Landmark in 1980.

Lew Wallace Elementary is now a vital part of downtown Albuquerque. It is surrounded by law offices and courthouses, and is within walking distance of museums, parks, the zoo, and live theatre. We are so landlocked that in order to make room for our new library, gym, and cafeteria addition, we had to give up our parking lot!

Lew Wallace Elementary is a community magnet school. We believe if we involve children in community projects throughout their elementary school years, they will exit fifth grade with an embedded understanding that public service is a noble calling.

Staff turnover at our school is minimal, but does come around every two to three years due to teacher relocation or retirement. There is a calmness and a special feeing to our school. Employees comment that Lew Wallace Elementary has been a "haven" for them as they weather the storms of life. Students understand and adhere to behavioral expectations. Discipline consists of giving students a "red ticket," or a discipline notice, they must take home and get signed in addition to missing the next day's recesses. Fifth graders still play tag together, and parents are greeted on a first-name basis when they walk in the door. The school climate is such that visitors often point out to our faculty that this is something rare and refreshing.

This wasn't always the case. Upon my arrival at Lew Wallace (13 years ago), I had the staff brainstorm critical issues most in need of attention, and the top two were discipline and lack of parent involvement. We have come a long way. The climate of our school did not improve on its own. It has been nurtured and is a result of intentional choices made by all of us who work there. As in anything else, we believe we can accomplish what we choose to accomplish, while working with what is within our circle of control.

Interestingly enough, during that brainstorming session 13 years ago, instruction and assessment were not even on the list generated by teachers. Truth be told, our school has always had dedicated, knowledgeable, and experienced teachers.

Quality teaching has always been in place, and student learning has always been evident. We were making adequate yearly progress and as a staff believed we were doing all the right things. But as one of our third-grade teachers likes to put it, "You don't know what you don't know."

## WHEN SUMMATIVE ASSESSMENT IS NOT ENOUGH

Implementing formative assessments has transformed our school. Before that, we were by all accounts a progressive school with a traditional grading system. The majority of assessments administered by classroom teachers were summative in nature, and typically came after completion of a chapter or at the end of a unit of study. Their purpose was so teachers could have a grade for their grade book, and students would know where they stood in class. The challenge with this process lay in the finality of it all. Once a student received the grade, he or she accepted the grade and everyone could move on to the next assignment or project, and the cycle would begin all over again. Feedback, if given at all, was minimal, and while it may have been somewhat informative, it was not timely enough for a student to apply the advice to his next piece of work or the work that had already been graded. When this type of summative assessment is not balanced with any formative assessment, it can nurture within a student a passiveness toward his learning. If only one opportunity to demonstrate knowledge is provided, then a student will most likely lose ownership of his ability to make the necessary decisions to move his learning forward. This puts the student in a position of accepting someone else's sole opinion about his capabilities, which in turn can foster limitations.

When referring to the traditional grading system that existed at our school, teachers have said that they often lacked the confidence and knowledge to thoroughly explain a child's grades to parents during parent-teacher conferences. Of course, they had plenty of graded assignments and could speak to a child's level of motivation and class participation, but what was missing were set criteria that would justify why the grade had been given in the first place. Rubrics were virtually nonexistent, and proficiency was not defined. This was acceptable to parents because this was all that they had ever known themselves. To add to the vagueness of it all, the limited amount of collaboration between classroom teachers regarding student work led to a subjective lens through which grading occurred. Nothing was in place to ensure that the "A" given in one classroom meant the same as the "A" given in another. A teacher in the primary grades recently shared she would always begin her parent-teacher conferences with the report card faced down as it did not support, but rather hindered, her efforts to explain a student's progress to parents.

One of the biggest drawbacks of the traditional assessment system we had in place was that it lacked both the depth and process to measure what students *really* knew. Many pieces of information made their way into the mix and resulted in the final grade as it was transferred from the grade book onto the report card. Some of it was clearly not reflective of a student's true knowledge: zeros for homework not turned in, assignments "graded down" because they had been turned in late, and strictly one-size-fits-all paper-and-pencil tests that addressed only one type of learner. Average it all together and a muddy view of student progress would emerge.

Concerned teachers look to colleagues for advice when a student is struggling in their classroom. Certainly this occurred before we began our work with formative assessments. However, collaborating about the progress of a single student is far different than collaborating about the progress of *all* students. It was just not imaginable that teacher A would ever score teacher B's students' writing to determine proficiency across the grade level. Each teacher's students "belonged" to that teacher alone. It was inconceivable that classroom teachers would work together to create authentic assessments, give constructive feedback to each other as professionals, or brainstorm to reach consensus on strategies that would move students to proficiency. Proficiency was not a part of our vocabulary. Simply put, classroom teachers were on their own without the support of a collaborative team.

Before formative assessments, we were just not working in a standards-based system. Programs and textbooks drove our curriculum, and our assessments were tests given for accountability purposes rather than for diagnosing and prescribing. The focus was on the product rather than the learner. All of that would change with the work of Douglas Reeves and The Leadership and Learning Center.

## FORMATIVE ASSESSMENT ARRIVES

In the fall of 2003, Douglas Reeves was invited to speak to the principals in our district on the topic of "Why Standards Matter." As I listened to him, I knew somehow I would need to figure out how to bring his message to my staff, and that his work was something we would need to begin to look at together. This opportunity presented itself when our then superintendent invited schools to pilot the Standards Based Progress Report (SBPR). The plan was that eventually all elementary schools would use this tool as the method of reporting student progress to families. Our superintendent recognized this type of reporting would be in conflict with the traditional letter grades for students in the intermediate grades and check pluses and minuses for children in the primary grades. She was wise in appreciating all it would entail for teachers and administrators to create a system of authentic assessment that parents and students could understand and support. It made sense to begin with a few schools, and it made sense to ask for volunteers.

Taking this request to the teachers at my school, I asked the question, "Are we ready to implement this new method of reporting to our families, and if we are not ready, what do we have to do to get ready?" Of course, I knew we weren't, but I needed them to recognize that for themselves without me telling them. After much discussion, everyone came to consensus that we were not ready and that we had a lot of work to do before we ever would be. Grade levels then met to brainstorm ideas of what they needed in order to be prepared to implement the district Standards Based Progress Report. The following is a breakdown of what they came up with:

*Kindergarten and first-grade teachers*

- Create rubrics (grade level, primary, intermediate)
- Study groups (tap resources from other schools)
- Cross-grade-level collaboration
- Dialogue with parents

*Second- and third-grade teachers*

- School-wide professional development
- Develop rubrics/assessments for consistency
- Time needed to understand language of progress report
- Help parents to understand new grading system
- Utilize math and literacy study groups to study assessments

*Fourth- and fifth-grade teachers*

- More time to study and develop and understand rubrics
- School-wide professional development around the implementation of standards
- Educating parents
- More information on actual progress report
- Staff needs to study implementation of standards (collaboration, professional development, study groups)

This was the response I was looking for, and one that would open the door to what was to be a great journey of professional learning for all of us at Lew Wallace Elementary. The awareness had been raised, and once we began, there was no turning back!

In the fall of 2003, I introduced the staff to Douglas Reeves' book *Making Standards Work: How to Implement Standards-Based Assessments in the Classroom, School, and District* (2002b). We read it together in a study-group format so all of us could be on the same page. In addition, every staff member who dealt with instruction in any way—classroom teachers, support staff, educational assistants, administration—was able to hear Douglas Reeves speak twice as he spoke of the importance of nonfiction writing, rubrics, Power Standards, and giving students multiple opportunities for success. Together, all of us viewed his tapes and discussed what applying those practices would mean to our school. We were, through all of this, developing a common language around standards-based instruction and assessment.

Around this time, Lew Wallace Elementary, along with the 13 other schools that at the time made up the Albuquerque High Cluster, came together to create a system for authentic assessment that would be referred to as the Albuquerque High Cluster Writing Portfolio. The composition of these schools included 10 elementary schools, two middle schools, and one high school. Over a period of eight years, teachers and administrators from these schools met monthly to create common grade-level rubrics in the area of nonfiction writing. In addition, this committee was charged with developing a plan schools could follow to help them assess student effort, progress, and achievement toward specific writing standards.

It was our school's introduction to the use of rubrics. We discovered that while developing and using rubrics took more time, they were a more accurate way of measuring student progress. At this point, we made the decision as a staff to create our own grade-level rubrics separate from the cluster ones. We were taking baby steps into the world of true collaboration! Once grade levels completed their rubrics, we came together to give each other feedback in an effort to determine the specificity and accuracy of the rubrics. We learned from studying Douglas Reeves' book that as professionals we had to be willing to do what we ask students to do when we ask for rewrites. He taught us that a strong rubric would require revisions. Nevertheless, it took courage on the part of teachers to step into the unknown—that of telling colleagues their rubric needed work and the criteria were not clear. While it was at first awkward for teachers to provide constructive criticism to one another, it was equally unpleasant for teachers to receive it. This was new territory for us and we could have easily turned back with our egos intact. Instead we forged ahead, eventually becoming more and more comfortable with this new process, and even learning to jointly laugh at ourselves through our learning curve.

## PERFORMANCE ASSESSMENTS CHANGE OUR WORLD

There were many, many steps that we took on our quest to bring formative assessment to our school, none of which was more important than bringing Lisa Almeida from The Leadership and Learning Center to work with us. Over the course of three years, Lisa guided us through the implementation of powerful best practices that build upon each other. The practices include (in the order that we implemented them):

- Identifying Power Standards
- "Unwrapping" standards, "Big Ideas," and "Essential Questions"
- Performance Assessments

As we started this work, our instructional coach, Stephanie Lovato, and I decided it was important to go slowly so as a staff we could develop a *deep* understanding of standards-based education of which formative assessment is a key piece. Going slowly was important because it would keep staff from becoming overwhelmed or anxious, as can be the case when something new is introduced in a school. We had two mantras: "It's a process!" and "Progress, not perfection." Our staff needed to understand that this was not something that was going to happen overnight. This type of reassurance relieved teachers of any apprehension that might otherwise have interfered with their learning.

When it came time to identifying Power Standards in all content areas, staff members were divided up into grade spans, including support staff (physical education teacher, librarian, technology, and reading teachers), as well as educational assistants and myself. It took several months of staff meetings and designated collaboration time for the work to get done, but the vertical articulation that occurred among staff was invaluable. Through this process, teachers became familiar not just with their own grade-level standards but with the previous and following grade-level standards as well.

When we moved on to "unwrapping" the standards and determining Big Ideas and Essential Questions, staff worked by grade levels and support staff paired off with different grades. This, too, proved a lengthy, but *oh so* very worthwhile, process. Teachers declare this step as one of the most important ones of all. They shared that the "unwrapping" made instruction more focused, more manageable, and clarified the essential skills and concepts they needed to teach as well as integrate across the curriculum. Daniel DelaO, first-grade teacher, commented at the time, "The process of 'unwrapping' standards has given me a systematic lesson plan template, if you will. Having a Power Standards template for my lessons ensures my instruction is prioritized and precise." Standards were no longer "fuzzy." They were truly understood.

Second-grade teacher Pam Porter explained it best: "The process I went through the year of identifying and then 'unwrapping' Power Standards supports the notion students can gain more from depth than breadth. The focus on critical skills and how these skills are upwardly articulated allows for greater coordination of skills and content (K–5) and lessens the possibilities of gaps in education."

While a few individuals could have identified the Power Standards and "unwrapped" them for the school, thus saving everyone a tremendous amount of time, the true professional development piece that can only be gained when there is participation in the process would have been lost on all but a few. In addition, because these processes were completed in grade spans rather than by having grade levels work in isolation, everyone had a better understanding of what content and skills were to be taught at each grade level. We discovered that if we were going to be true to working within a standards-based system, everyone would need to be able to articulate the work being done.

These processes were indeed lengthy in nature. A teacher recently expressed, at the time we were meeting regularly on a weekly basis, and sometimes two times a week, there was so much information to discuss and so many voices to hear, we had to commit to a regular schedule so that we could get everything done that we needed to. During these meetings, faculty members were allowed to process and ask questions. Concepts were explained and reexplained. We knew by now there were no shortcuts to this important work. We were relentless in our determination to get each step down, before moving to the next one.

Once we had the foundational pieces of standards-based education strongly embedded at our school, we posed the question to Lisa Almeida, "OK, Lisa, what's the next step?" Without any hesitation, she said the two words that would change teaching, learning, and assessment at our school forever: "Performance Assessments." She told us, "These will get you the biggest bang for your buck!"

We were to discover that Performance Assessments (PAs) have to be one of the most powerful teaching and assessment tools of all time! Units of study, they are based on "unwrapped" Power Standards and supporting standards. The units are composed of four to five tasks that increase in rigor as they move from one task to the next. Each task has its own rubric that allows for self-assessment and provides immediate feedback for students as well as teachers. Before a student can advance to a different task, he must first be proficient on the current one. This process allows for instruction to be differentiated for students needing additional support between tasks. The level of engagement from English Language Learners, students with disabilities, students in a gifted program, and all students in general has been tremendous.

The work with Performance Assessments at our school began with two classroom teachers, Stephanie, and myself. Since Stephanie and I were learning about these assessments right along with the teachers, it made sense not to take this initiative to all of the staff at once. The two teachers received tremendous support: time to prepare their assessments, supplies, and constant feedback from Stephanie, Lisa, and me. It was impossible to restrain the excitement that started coming from those two classrooms. One teacher commented that Performance Assessments call on higher-level thinking, and she could now see what her students were capable of producing when given the opportunity. Sharing their work at staff meetings brought a high level of enthusiasm to the rest of the staff. What was particularly exciting was how quiet or reserved students were taking the spotlight and running away with these engaging assessments. High-level student participation and motivation was selling all of us on Performance Assessments. It was time for Lisa to provide training for the rest of the staff.

From the moment teachers began creating and implementing their own Performance Assessments, there was never any hesitation in supporting them in any and every way possible. They were encouraged and supported with constant assurance and reassurance. They received coverage for their classroom if they wanted to work on designing a PA, or stipends were offered if they preferred to work after school. If a teacher needed assistance with her students during a task, I would find another staff member or volunteer my time to go into the classroom and help out. If teachers needed supplies, all they had to do was ask for them. Whatever they needed was made available to them. This work was still new and it was necessary to keep the momentum going to prevent discouragement or resistance.

## PARENTS JOIN THE TEAM

As our district began rolling out the Standards Based Progress Report in lieu of the standardized report card, pilot schools found themselves feeling the pushback from parents. Teachers at those schools also found themselves struggling with explaining the language, content, and format of the new progress report. A district survey taken by a consulting firm reported recommendations for the SBPR ranging from wanting "clearer definitions of achievement" to "needs better marketing." *Yet this was not the case with our school.*

In an effort to recruit parent support in this massive paradigm shift to a standards-based educational system, the district allowed parents to vote for accepting the sole use of standards-based marks (4, 3, 2, 1) or going with *both* standards-based *and* traditional letter grades (A, B, C, D, F). District policy required that schools have the consent of two-thirds of their family community to transition to standards-based marks only. When it came time for our school community to vote, the response came back with 81 percent ready to give up letter grades! We became the first official school of 88 elementary schools to be able to roll out the SBPR without letter grades. What had we done to receive such a response? Simply put, we had chosen to do the work necessary to understand operating in a standards-based system instead of piloting a progress report we were unprepared to speak to. Through identifying Power Standards, "unwrapping" standards, determining Big Ideas and Essential Questions, and utilizing rubrics and Performance Assessments as formative assessment tools, we were becoming fluent in the language of standards, so our conversations with parents and community members were based on knowledge, not assumptions, emotions, or myths. This was key.

It was important that as we were "building our new house," we were sharing our blueprint with our families. These are the steps that we took. First, parents were introduced to the use of rubrics. Rubrics began accompanying homework assignments so that parents could clearly understand what was expected of students. In addition, teachers used rubrics during parent-teacher conferences to explain student strengths and areas of need in nonfiction writing in a manner that made sense to them. Teachers began posting their rubrics and standards in the hallway along with student work. They worked in teams to develop attractive and informational brochures about grade-level Power Standards and shared them with families at Open House. Classroom newsletters always included the standards that a class was currently studying, and an overview of a Performance Assessment was included if one was being implemented at the time.

In October 2006, we held a Standards-Based Education Night where Lisa Almeida explained to families the components of a standards-based system. Teachers were present to share firsthand experiences. The event concluded with a gallery walk of Performance Assessments and binders containing student work that students could speak to. This was followed at a later date with a Standard-Based Assessment Night where we invited a representative from the district's department of Research, Development, and Accountability to describe the new state assessment and how it differed from the previous norm-referenced one. It stands to reason that by the time parents at our school were given Standards Based Progress Report ballots and asked to cast their vote, they understood what the staff had concluded only a short time before them, that giving letter grades to students in a standards-based environment would be like working within two different and separate systems.

## KEEPING A SINGLE FOCUS

It is easy for educators to be pulled in many directions. There are federal, state, district, and school expectations/mandates. Principals have an obligation to teachers to make sure all of these requirements are aligned, so when starting something new, teachers are able to stay focused on the new initiative. Schools in our state are required to have an Educational Plan for Student Success (EPSS) to ensure students are receiving the support necessary to meet or exceed standards. In addition, all certified teachers must have a Professional Development Plan (PDP) in place every year to document growth in the areas of instruction, student learning, and professional learning. When we began our work in standards-based instruction and assessment, we made sure these plans were reflective of the changes we were undertaking at our school. This way, no one ever felt like they were jumping from one thing to another, trying to learn and implement a variety of things at once. We were keeping the "main thing the main thing." Our librarian, Cheryl Inskeep, put it this way: "The school-wide focus aligned with our PDPs. Working together as a team, we shared a common experience and produced a similar vocabulary."

## STANDARDS DRIVE
## INSTRUCTION AND ASSESSMENT

No one ever said change is easy, and change for the sake of change alone is not enough. When thought out and purposeful, however, change can be both exciting and rewarding. At our school when we began this journey, we were naïve about the depth of change that would occur within ourselves as professionals and within our school as a whole. It took a lot of work, and work that wasn't easy or always pleasant. People are always going to be in different places in their professional and personal lives, thereby slowing down the process and at times risking its success. There were times when Stephanie and I both just wanted to walk away. But because we stayed the course, and teachers made the commitment to stay right along with us, our school is a "true" standards-based school with standards-based classrooms where standards are the driver for daily instruction and assessment. We have *earned* the right to this claim.

We have come a long way from being timid and offended when giving or receiving feedback on each other's assessments or instruction. Through the process we have learned it's not about the adults as much as it is about the students. Teachers are very comfortable pointing out to each other why a student's writing piece is a "3" and not a "4" and why their formative assessment needs rewording so students "get" what is being asked of them. Together we work at revising rubrics and Performance Assessments, always aiming for uncompromising clarity. One teacher says it very well when she says, "I'm learning to think like a third grader!" The exchange of ideas, brainstorming of strategies, charting grade-level data, and learning from one another describes the transformational change that has occurred within us. Collaboration with a purpose is a gift, and one that now defines the culture of our school.

Throughout this chapter, I have made reference to the importance of all parties sharing a common language. This means that the principal, teachers, students, parents, and the custodian all understand what is meant by a rubric and a Performance Assessment. This was demonstrated a few years ago when a teacher was preparing information to send home regarding the school-wide science fair. Without missing a beat, the *school secretary* pointed out to him that he had left out rubrics as part of the packet, thereby making it difficult for students to understand the requirements for their science projects. Since then the science fair has been completely revamped. It no longer makes sense to award ribbons to first, second, and third place winners. It does make sense to provide ribbons to all students who reach a proficient or exemplary rating according to the criteria set forth by the rubric. Students have learned to be advocates of their learning. They will not hesitate in pointing out why their project should have been scored differently when they do not agree with the judge's score. They use the rubric to state their case, and we welcome their questioning. Since science fair judges are individuals from the business community, they too have had to be educated in this new way that we do things. The point is that there are no mysteries or misunderstandings with rubrics. Students and parents know what is expected in a project, and when completed, they also know why the project was scored as it was. These changes to our school were not planned but rather evolved as we left one system and moved into the next. For example, when it came time for the annual awards ceremony we have at the end of every school year, teachers realized certificates of achievement needed to reflect proficiency and exemplary levels instead of grade point averages.

I don't think anything brings more excitement to students than Performance Assessments, and it carries over to the adults in their lives as well. Students work with them from kindergarten through fifth grade. Teachers must endure the constant question posed to them by the students in their class: "When are we going to work on our PAs?" If it were up to them, Performance Assessments would be what they would do all day, every day. Teachers have commented, "I wish I could teach this way all the time." The defining characteristics of Performance Assessments are high student engagement, immediate feedback, and a diagnostic tool for teachers as well as students, opportunities for writing that matters, as well as multiple opportunities for success. In addition, they cover a multitude of skills and standards. They have it all. Especially rewarding for teachers is that by design Performance Assessments follow Bloom's six levels of cognitive processes so *all* students are offered the opportunity to experience all levels of learning. Students who require more time to grasp a concept also need to use higher-level thinking skills, and students more advanced in their learning deserve to be challenged and not limited to lower-level thinking tasks. To visualize the varied academic advantages of Performance Assessments, see Exhibit 6.1.

Marcia Ortiz, third-grade teacher, recently shared, "You see the joy in their faces when I tell them to go get their Performance Assessment binder." Imagine, joy of learning! Parents, too, come into the classroom and inform teachers of how good students feel about this work. The level of engagement is priceless. A special education teacher at our school recently shared that a student in her class had earned 15 minutes of "free time." When asked how she would like to use it, she replied, "Can I get a laptop so I can work on my Performance Assessment?" This level of engagement can be seen 10 times over in classroom after classroom at our school. It is still an anomaly to us that students never complain about rewrites when working on a PA. Perhaps it is the constant feedback that they are receiving or the modified one-on-one instruction that they get when their teacher discovers the need to introduce a task in a different way. Studying the work of Douglas Reeves, we learned that it is

 **EXHIBIT 6.1** **Benefits of Performance Assessments**

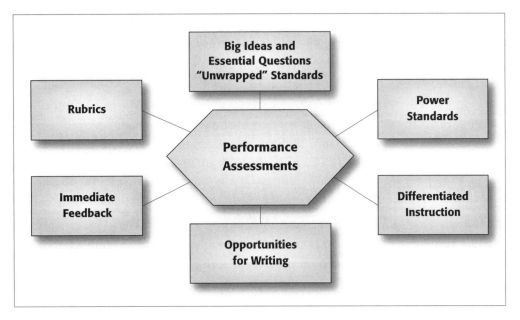

important to always give students something worth writing about. Performance Assessments always include meaningful writing. Maybe that is the key and what makes the difference to students.

When asked about formative assessments in her kindergarten class, Cheryl Wheeler said, "Rubrics and Performance Assessments are very helpful. They provide that immediate feedback so many of us are struggling to find time to give to students. The great thing about these two resources is they require little of the teachers because students just take them and run with them. This shows me that students are taking ownership of their own learning. The group of students I have this year seems to be my lowest-performing group of all time, yet they are devouring my PAs. I can't explain why. I'm not really doing anything different. These students just really like knowing their goals and going after them."

What I am certain about is this. Performance Assessments have and will continue to endure the test of time. Budget cuts may come, and they have. In this time of financial educational crisis, we may have fewer personnel at schools than we would like, and we have faced that, too. Nevertheless, Performance Assessments continue to flourish at our school. I believe that is because they give us the results we are after in the form of improved student skills, and also because of the components that make up a PA. Power Standards, "unwrapped" standards, Essential Questions, Big Ideas, rubrics, timely feedback, and multiple opportunities for success are all important pieces of standards-based instruction and assessment.

Jude Edwards, third-grade teacher, explains it like this: "Creating my own Performance Assessment has allowed me to use everything I've learned from the beginning of our study on standards-based education: selecting grade-level standards, 'unwrapping' them, creating rubrics, utilizing Bloom's Taxonomy hierarchy of thinking skills, Gardner's multiple intelligences, the step-by-step process, and the squared planning tool that Lisa Almeida from The Center introduced us to. It feels good to use what I've learned and be able to apply it. In my twenty-two years of teaching, I can honestly and proudly say learning about and creating and implementing Performance Assessments remains my biggest accomplishment."

Granted, a strong, worthwhile Performance Assessment takes time and discipline to create. Like a rubric, it will most likely require modifications once it is implemented. It can change from year to year depending on the class. Teachers say that students themselves remain their greatest teachers. Students change the PAs themselves. They take tasks to the next level. They make suggestions. A teacher recently commented, "When you create a Performance Assessment, you just have to be on fire about it. You want it to be 'meaty and rich.' When I complete one like this, I feel fabulous! Yet even then, I know once the students and I began working with it, it will change because the students themselves will improve it. Performance Assessments in my classroom allow for all of us, students and myself, to become equal facilitators of their learning."

## REFLECTING ON THE PROCESS

A principal cannot bring systemic change to a school without the help of others. Stephanie Lovato, instructional coach, was someone who shared my vision from the beginning and stood with me when few others would have. The work I have written about in this chapter would not have happened to the extent and the level that it did if either one of us had not been present throughout the whole process. Together we studied, planned, and facilitated. We brought two different perspectives to the process and allowed those differences to strengthen our work instead of take away from it. It was, after all, not about us, but about our school and the guidance we could provide to teachers as they embraced working in this *very different* type of system.

Even then, we realized that there was training that needed to occur that we were not qualified to provide. We were very protective of staff and insisted they have only the best possible training from those we considered experts in their field. We could not have anyone mistakenly undo what we had worked so hard to create. Lisa Almeida and the work of The Leadership and Learning Center were those teachers. Educators particularly appreciated Lisa's professional yet approachable style. Her clear, precise manner of explaining the process allowed all of us to believe we could replicate it for ourselves.

I also came to realize the importance of knowing when to step back so teachers could step up and take the lead. Ultimately, it is, after all, only they who can make the decision whether to take ownership of the professional development offered to them.

First-grade teacher Daniel DelaO recently reflected, "It's been poignant and eye opening to see the impressive body of work we have accomplished. It reminds me of the rigor of college master's level work. At this school we have gone beyond the study group and taken it to teacher research in motion. Our work with Performance Assessments is just that, teacher research in action."

A process such as the one we undertook from strictly summative to a balance of both formative and summative assessment cannot exist solely on the surface. It must be deeply understood and embedded in the culture of the school. It cannot be rushed and steps cannot be skipped. Professional development must be differentiated for staff and information presented time and time again. Teachers must be supported at whatever level they are at in their understanding of new concepts. I knew teachers would move at different rates, but the expectation was that all would make progress. No one person could do the work for another. For this level of change to occur, teachers had to experience every step for themselves. In our case, it was these actions that both created and strengthened the foundational structure of what is instruction and assessment in our school today.

We did not set out to redefine assessment at our school. We simply set out to learn about implementing a standards-based system. Along the way, we discovered such implementation would require the involvement of everyone at our school, including students and parents. Through the process we undertook of examining and discussing standards, collaboratively determining proficiency levels, and examining student work, we realized that our way of grading and assessing no longer made sense. In a way, formative assessment found us.

Cheryl Wheeler, kindergarten teacher, sums it up: "For me, it's all about assessment. I assess to see how my students are doing and how *I'm* doing. I use the outcomes of the assessments to identify what skills I need to teach/reteach, and how I then need to differentiate my instruction for them. I use assessment outcomes to create my small groups for center instruction where they then receive individualized attention daily. We practice, practice, and practice the skill(s) they need in short bursts and with various methods. DRA2, although a summative assessment, is also used to identify student needs. I fill out the continuum on the back and identify strategies that will help my students move forward. This step also helps me realize what I need to focus on with reading instruction. For example, with one group I know I need to work on more retelling strategies. Most of the students have broken the reading code, but of course need more practice to build fluency. Some students, on the other hand, who are fluent readers lack comprehension. It varies, which means I vary my teaching—thus differentiated instruction. This is why I feel so strongly that formative assessment is critical. It tells us what we need to do, how we need to do it, and what the students need! It's just too easy, too perfect!"

For us, formative assessment has meant that now all students have a chance to finish the race. I am grateful that as a staff we chose to step outside of our comfort zone and, with the help of Lisa Almeida, discover a way to help every student at our school experience excitement, confidence, and success while becoming "captains of their own ship of learning" (Brookhart, 1996).

I thank those teachers who courageously reflected on their teaching practice and through great determination studied, listened, questioned, debated, laughed, cried, analyzed, and transformed their work with the most honorable of intentions. I recognize Stephanie Lovato, Daniel DelaO, Jude Edwards, Marcia Ortiz, Terry Vargas, Rebecca Griego, Cheryl Wheeler, Christina Orozco, Ali Nava, Cheryl Inskeep, Catherine McCabe, Betty Montano, Alvie Torres, Javonna George, and Stephanie Kasprzak. As they continue to learn from their students, I will continue to learn from them.

# | | | | **GETTING REAL...** | | | |

As you reflect on Lew Wallace's real-time decisions, think about how their story applies to you in your current setting, and then answer the following questions:

1. *"When this type of summative assessment is not balanced with any formative assessment, it can nurture within a student a passiveness toward his learning. If only one opportunity to demonstrate knowledge is provided, then a student will most likely lose ownership of his ability to make the necessary decisions to move his learning forward."*

   How many opportunities do your students have to demonstrate mastery at school? Does this differ by subject? By teacher? By grade level? Is the feedback mostly summative, formative, or would you say there is a balance? Explain.

   _____

   _____

   _____

   _____

2. *"However, collaborating about the progress of a single student is far different than collaborating about the progress of* all *students."*

   How does collaboration currently look in your setting? Do you have a systematic way to meet in teams and discuss the needs of all children, or is it much more on an individual basis?

   _____

   _____

   _____

   _____

3. *"Before formative assessments, we were just not working in a standards-based system. Programs and textbooks drove our curriculum, and our assessments were tests given for accountability purposes rather than for diagnosing and prescribing. The focus was on the product rather than the learner."*

What drives your system? Products, programs, and textbooks or the learner? What evidence do you have to support your conclusion?

_____

_____

_____

_____

4. The focus on improving the instruction and learning taking place at Lew Wallace ended up increasing overall parental interest and involvement in their children's education.

It would have been easy for the principal to take the early assessment of faculty members where they determined the top needs of the school (parental involvement being one of the top two) and turn them into separate initiatives (e.g., What can we do to increase parental involvement?). However, she chose to focus on the students' instructional needs, and the parental involvement flowed from that. What is your reaction to this result?

_____

_____

_____

_____

5. *"This was demonstrated a few years ago when a teacher was preparing information to send home regarding the school-wide science fair. Without missing a beat, the* school secretary *pointed out to him he had left out rubrics as part of the packet, thereby making it difficult for students to understand the requirements for their science projects."*

Is your secretary (or any other member of the support staff at your site) keenly aware of what initiatives you are implementing and the meaning behind the jargon surrounding them? What does the secretary's response say about the culture and belief system at Lew Wallace? Do you feel this level of involvement is important? Why or why not?

_____

_____

_____

_____

# CHAPTER SEVEN

# Carroll County Middle School
## Carrollton, Kentucky

*"The most important transformation that took place at CCMS involved the conversations that took place among the staff. The staff developed a cohesiveness and focus on expectations of student learning in relation to the standards. These conversations did not take place in isolation, as was the case previously. In one conversation, a new teacher described the reason that students did not score well on the CFA: 'I did not get them there, this was an area of weakness for me as a teacher.' WOW! A first-year teacher feeling safe enough with her peers to admit her own weaknesses. Imagine what then took place in that meeting as experienced teachers shared what they had done with students as they taught the same content; this sounds like job-embedded professional development."*

—Bill Hogan, Former Principal of CCMS

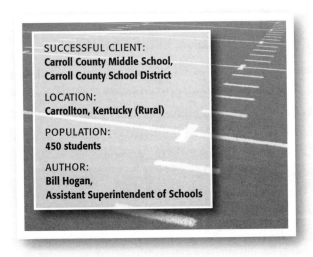

SUCCESSFUL CLIENT:
**Carroll County Middle School,
Carroll County School District**

LOCATION:
**Carrollton, Kentucky (Rural)**

POPULATION:
**450 students**

AUTHOR:
**Bill Hogan,
Assistant Superintendent of Schools**

# OUR SCHOOL

Carrollton, Kentucky, sits at the confluence of the Ohio and Kentucky Rivers. While it is a rural community, we are situated 45 minutes from both Louisville and Cincinnati, and one hour from Lexington. We are home to many industries, such as Dow Corning, North American Stainless, and Kentucky Utilities.

Following are some key facts about Carroll County Middle School:

- 450 students in grades 6–8
- 65% free and reduced lunch students
- 8% minority, mostly consisting of Hispanic students
- Offers Read 180, Read Naturally for reading intervention
- Carnegie Learning for math grades 7–8
- Offers algebra I to students in grades 7 and 8 who have shown ability to master content
- Offers geometry to eighth-grade students who have shown mastery of content at grade level
- Use of Thinklink from Discovery Education as Interim Benchmark Assessment for reading, math, science, and social studies
- Students have 80 minutes of math and reading every day at all levels
- Two math and two language arts teachers at each grade level
- Teams have common planning, 40 minutes for individual planning and 40 minutes for team planning
- Gaps in both free and reduced population and special education

# WHERE WE STARTED

When my administrative team began at Carroll County Middle School during the summer of 2003, our school was one of the lowest-performing schools in the region. Kentucky is separated into educational cooperative regions. These cooperatives provide assistance to districts in their area by providing resources, professional development, and other types of support. Carroll County belongs to the Ohio Valley Educational Cooperative (OVEC).

Students in the state of Kentucky take the Commonwealth Accountability Test. This assessment of learning is taken in April of each school year and then schools receive their scores the following October. With this amount of lag time, three months of the new school year have been completed before we receive the results, making it almost impossible to craft immediate changes to curriculum. We hope this problem will be alleviated with the new Core Standards and new testing system in place for next year, but that is not within our control. The adult actions in each classroom are, and that is the focus of this chapter.

The scores we received for the 2002/03 school year were not good. In the areas of reading and math, the school had 45 percent proficient or distinguished in reading and 16 percent proficient or distinguished in mathematics. Our free and reduced lunch students' scores were much worse, with only 37 percent scoring proficient or distinguished in reading and 5 percent scoring proficient or distinguished in math. This placed our school near the bottom of the OVEC region. As a matter of fact, we were 20 out of 22 when compared to the other middle schools in OVEC. Our region has diverse school systems, some wealthy, some poor, some urban, some rural, so it is not comparing apples to oranges. It was a good comparison and legitimate.

## The Staff in the Beginning

The staff at Carroll County Middle School was hardworking. Many were as dedicated as I witnessed in other schools. You could also identify some teachers who were not carrying their loads, which is a situation I am sure everyone can find in their own setting. As a first-year principal coming right from the classroom, I knew I would have to lean on my administrative team for support and guidance. One of the many shockers I received was in my first weeks on the job.

I sent a note to teachers to let them know how excited I was about being a team member at CCMS, and told them the administrative team would love to sit down with them in the next few weeks to discuss their plans for the year, previous lesson plans or upcoming lesson plans, unit mapping, and an assessment—all items I thought teachers would have at their fingertips. However, the note I received just one week later from someone on staff indicated the uphill climb that was to come.

The letter started so kindly: *"We are glad you are with us, we understand you are young,"* it read. However, the tone changed with the all-too-familiar word *but*. It then moved on to some phrases that only a seasoned, salty veteran English Lit person could write: *"What is this, the calling of the guard to his royal highness' throne?"* (Doesn't that sound like someone who has studied European Literature?) The note went on to say I would have many other things going on during the first few weeks of school, which would keep me too busy to worry about what teachers were doing in their classrooms. Imagine an instructional leader worrying about "other" things than what goes on in the classroom! It was signed by the Committee to Prevent Unnecessary Work when None is Needed. I couldn't reconcile the scores we produced with the need not to do this work!

# THE CLIMB

Change is slow. If you have been in the school business, you know this is an understatement. I do not believe there is one magic bullet that will fix all the problems facing education; however, there is a systematic way of doing business in schools that leads to great success. With all of the products out there claiming to be the way to change schooling for the better, we have to be careful what we select to pursue in the name of improvement.

The focus of our first year together was getting to know each other, and we worked hard at developing lesson plans and knowing where we were going with our students from day to day and week by week. My leadership team believed strongly in the power of planning for teachers, and we felt that some of them were not doing this effectively. With our focus and determination, we made strides our first year together; however, we lost quite a few veterans from our staff in the process.

## The First Step

While still a teacher, I was afforded the opportunity to attend the Kentucky Leadership Academy. During one session, I was introduced to the work of Richard and Rebecca DuFour. At the time I did not understand the impact the book *Professional Learning Communities* would have on my philosophy as a building administrator. There was an eighth-grade student during my first year as principal who made straight "A's," but scored at the lowest level on the state test. My question was, how did this happen? What did her grades reflect? The scores reflected the student worked hard and turned in assignments; unfortunately, she did not get the content at a mastery (or even developing) level. I felt we had failed her as a student and let her move to the high school unprepared. We did nothing extra or different to meet her needs.

To answer these questions, during my second year on the administrative team, I started to initiate conversations focused on the concepts discussed in the book *Professional Learning Communities at Work* (DuFour and Eaker, 1998). I did not specifically name the strategies we would put into place, but rather described why we needed to take these steps. I told staff about the student mentioned earlier, and that currently our school did not have a systematic way of responding to this student or anyone like her. We had to change this; we had to have a process in place to engage students beyond the normal classroom instruction that was taking place.

Our first attempt was crude; we created additional time for student learning after school. We called this session the "Safety Net after School Program." The program was established to help all students who were not completing work at the level needed, or just not completing the work at all. The staff would call the parents on the day the work was not turned in, so the student could stay that day to finish the assignment.

This conflicted with the philosophies of some of the teaching staff. My team heard faculty members complain about having to keep making copies of lost work. In addition, the staff was concerned they were working harder than the students to get work turned in, and felt we weren't teaching our students responsibility. The private and public conversations around these topics began the culture shift that was necessary to continue on our journey. We had to come to grips with the fact that by making the students complete the work no matter what, we were teaching them responsibility! The statement, "If it is important enough to assign, it is important enough to get back and give feedback on," was often voiced during faculty meetings.

## The Next Step

During our transition to Professional Learning Communities, we began discussing how we viewed data. Along with our current superintendent and former instructional supervisor, our school worked with The Leadership and Learning Center to instruct our staff members on the five-step Data Teams process. This session took place during the fall of that year and included the entire district. However, at the time, my focus was on my staff.

We had the framework complete. Professional Learning Communities forced us to address the issues and beliefs that if not scrutinized and worked through would prevent us from moving forward or making any progress at Carroll County Middle School. It was time to focus on looking at student work and creating a systematic way of improving teacher effectiveness. We had to quit offering one-shot professional development to teachers; they needed ongoing, job-embedded professional development. Our leadership team knew we had star teachers in our content areas, and it was our job to ensure their professional growth was fostered.

The Data Teams seminar was remarkable and opened the eyes of our staff members even wider. After the institute, we began implementing the Data Teams system with the goal of establishing a protocol for addressing areas in need of improvement in teaching and learning at CCMS. The need for Common Formative Assessments was one of the biggest take-aways from the instruction we received through The Leadership and Learning Center.

## The Final Step

With our team and meeting structure in place, grade-level team planning, the school culture, and the beliefs of our staff began to work together in what my leadership team felt was a critical component for achieving our goal of 100 percent proficient and distinguished. Common Formative Assessments (CFAs) were the final piece, and the key ingredient of the work we had to do. Our belief in the importance of CFAs was grounded in several mind-sets:

- Without Common Formative Assessments in place we could not guarantee to parents that students in one class were getting the same content as the class right next door.

- Mastery needed to be the same across content classrooms, and for every child.

- Conversations among teachers had to revolve around the results of our pre- and post-assessments.

- We had to be able to move students, if and when needed, to address areas of strength and weakness.

- We had to compare apples to apples.

One of the problems with having numerous teachers teaching the same subject is ensuring students are required to demonstrate proficiency of the same material. In our discussions with staff, we asked our teachers to imagine they were a parent who had twins. One was assigned to math teacher A, and the other sibling was assigned to math teacher B. And then we asked them, would their twins have equal access to the same material, and would their grades reflect common expectations of mastery of the work? These conversations were crucial in implementing CFAs. As a principal, the work of aligning mastery quizzes or tests across grade-level subjects is crucial. The dialogue among staff members at CCMS around aligning standards with the CFAs allowed our teachers to have deep discussions about the expectations of quality work, what each standard meant, and what teaching strategies would move students to our desired outcomes. Without Common Formative Assessments in place, I do not believe conversations among staff would have occurred to begin the true change in our school.

Monitoring the use of CFAs was important in the initial stages of implementation. Our math team decided to give mastery quizzes on Fridays of the material that was to be learned that week. The following Monday, the two members of the group would sit with my leadership team and discuss the results of the CFA from the preceding week. These discussions did not occur within the Data Teams structure, but rather were designed to be meetings with the intention of describing to me if our core instruction was meeting the needs of our students, and if it wasn't, what our plans were to address the issue. This method of monitoring allowed me to ensure conversations based on student learning were taking place, and every mathematics teacher knew the exact level of performance of each student in their class.

One of the struggles we had in the initial implementation was ensuring the CFAs matched the core content at the appropriate level. The Kentucky Department of Education established our state standards with depth of knowledge attached to each of them. We began truly monitoring and focusing on our assessment practices, and aligning questions to the appropriate level was often a time-intensive task. Through the Data Teams process, we were able to take advantage of teacher knowledge and build quality assessments that ensured that students were showing mastery at the appropriate depth of knowledge.

## AND THE RESULTS?

Remarkable! This one word describes the changes at CCMS since the implementation of CFAs. Again, our team did not and still does not believe this one change should be sufficient. The other steps and initiatives worked hand in hand to create this improvement. All the initiatives worked together to empower our school staff to modify and enhance what they were doing. In the words of our superintendent, Lisa James, "We have to have a laser-like focus on what we want students to know and be able to do."

We cannot talk about growth without discussing the results. As I mentioned at the beginning of this chapter, our scores in 2003 were not good. The following exhibits show the impact of the steps we took on student achievement. Exhibit 7.1 charts the growth in percentage of students scoring proficient or distinguished as measured by the Kentucky Commonwealth Accountability Test in Reading and Math. Exhibit 7.2 shows the percentage of free and reduced lunch students scoring proficient or distinguished on the same test.

As you can see, we did not reach our goal of 100 percent proficient or distinguished. However, we have made steady growth every year. One important side note, we did this with a steady rate of teacher turnover; in fact, in one of these years, four of our six mathematics teachers were new to the school, and the profession. Even after the departure of my leadership team, and the entrance of a new team, the school continued to show improvement. For all of this, we are extremely proud. Proud of our teachers, students, parents, and everyone else who supported us as we changed and implemented these transforming practices.

The most important transformation that took place at CCMS involved the conversations that took place among the staff. The staff developed a cohesiveness and focus on expectations of student learning in relation to the standards. These conver-

**EXHIBIT 7.1** Percentage of Students Scoring Proficient or Distinguished on the Kentucky Commonwealth Accountability Test in Reading and Math, 2003–2010

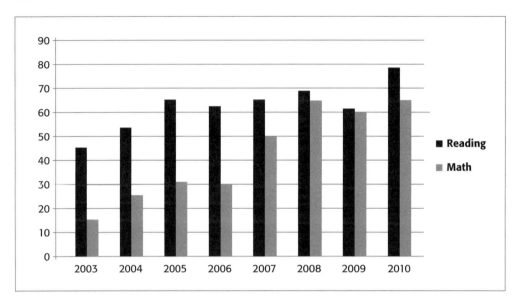

 **EXHIBIT 7.2** Percentage of Free and Reduced Lunch Students Scoring Proficient or Distinguished on the Kentucky Commonwealth Accountability Test in Reading and Math, 2003–2010

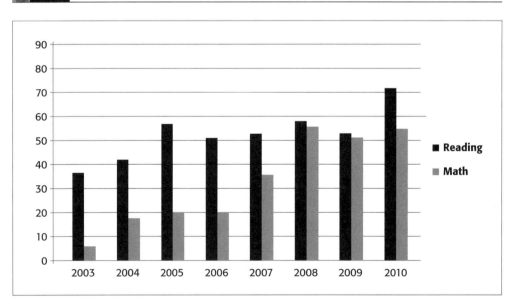

sations did not take place in isolation, as was the case previously. In one conversation, a new teacher described the reason that students did not score well on the CFA: "I did not get them there, this was an area of weakness for me as a teacher." WOW! A first-year teacher feeling safe enough with her peers to admit her own weaknesses. Imagine what then took place in that meeting as experienced teachers shared what they had done with students as they taught the same content; this sounds like job-embedded professional development.

As our sixth-grade math teacher, Nancy Simpson, stated, "Little did I know the intrinsic reward of how adding a green dot to weekly mastery check would be a contagious instructional motivator. After my coworker and I planned out weekly secure skills for evaluation, the reward of a green dot for mastery had my students literally eating out of my hands; it really bothered them when they did not earn the proficiency dot. The quest to please me was fostered by the opportunity to better themselves if at first they did not succeed. By striving to create common assessments that all students would complete, the reward was twofold—I got to know the exact performance level of my students, and they challenged each other to be the showcase classroom. A friendly competition jump-started the desire to learn, and the rewards were not bad either. Common assessments in my classroom were a win-win. It is just hard to say who got the better deal because I sharpened my assessment skills and they mastered sixth-grade math."

By taking the steps we have at Carroll County Middle School, we have seen and felt our culture shift. We have become responsive and systematic in teaching all students, from those who are advanced to the ones who are not progressing in the curriculum. Our scores have increased to a level such that only four middle schools in our area score higher. We owe our increases to the implementation of the PLC model, Data Teams, and Common Formative Assessments.

With the release of the Common Core Standards, and Kentucky's early adoption of those standards, we have an opportunity to grow further in our use of CFAs. Kentucky schools must have formative assessments established for all of the Core Standards by the beginning of the 2012 school year. Our previous work, and the culture we have fostered, will allow us to create these new assessments more efficiently and deliberately than we could have even just five short years ago.

| | | | **GETTING REAL...** | | | |

As you reflect on Carroll County Middle School's real-time decisions, think about how their story applies to you in your current setting, and then answer the following questions:

1. In his first few weeks as an administrator, Bill Hogan received a letter signed by the *Committee to Prevent Unnecessary Work When None is Needed.*

   Maybe this committee does not officially exist within your school or district; however, unofficially in any type of work environment, there is always someone who is prone to this sort of mentality. What strategies do you use to bring this type of person along when change must occur?

   _____

   _____

   _____

   _____

2. *"I do not believe there is one magic bullet that will fix all the problems facing education; however, there is a systematic way of doing business in schools that leads to great success. With all of the products out there claiming to be the way to change schooling for the better, we have to be careful what we select to pursue in the name of improvement."*

   In the past two years, what has your school or district pursued in the name of improvement? Were these choices right on target with the needs in your setting? Have they been implemented well?

   _____

   _____

   _____

   _____

3. *"It is just hard to say who got the better deal, because I sharpened my assessment skills and they mastered sixth-grade math."*

   This quote from an educator at CCMS shows the change that occurs through the implementation of Common Formative Assessments, not only when it comes to increasing student achievement, but also in the enhanced awareness of the power of educator practice. Are teaching skills growing at a parallel rate with student achievement scores in your setting? What evidence supports this conclusion?

_____

_____

_____

_____

4. *"Kentucky schools must have formative assessments established for all of the Core Standards by the beginning of the 2012 school year. Our previous work, and the culture we have fostered, will allow us to create these new assessments more efficiently and deliberately than we could have even just five short years ago."*

Common Formative Assessment is a powerful process that can be adapted to any change introduced within a school or district. When the educational course is altered within your setting, are the right processes and structures in place that allow for this type of flexibility? Explain.

_____

_____

_____

_____

CHAPTER EIGHT

# Berea Elementary School
## Montgomery, New York

*"Designing Common Formative Assessments as a Data Team has afforded us the experience to work collectively, guided by clear goals and deliberate evaluations to inform and guide our instruction. This process of using data has empowered our team in immeasurable ways. As a whole, our fourth-grade Data Team is more focused than ever on student learning and achievement. More importantly, we have become reenergized and empowered. We feel the future can only lead us to increased success."*

—Tracey Vianden, Special Education Teacher

SUCCESSFUL CLIENT:
**Berea Elementary School,
Valley Central School District**

LOCATION:
**Montgomery, New York (Suburban)**

POPULATION:
**425 students**

AUTHOR:
**Hope Stuart, Principal,
with support from Tracey Vianden,
Special Education Teacher**

# Berea Elementary School Depends on Deliberate Data to Drive Instruction

## DEMOGRAPHICS AND BACKGROUND

Berea Elementary School's 75 teachers and support staff are proud to service over 420 students spanning grades K through 5. Located approximately an hour north of New York City in the historic town of Montgomery, New York, Berea is one of five elementary schools within the Valley Central School District. Our dedicated and experienced teaching staff creates a warm, nurturing environment for our students, while maintaining high expectations for them. We believe our students will become creative and critical thinkers who will meet and exceed school district standards. With our building goals as our compass, we utilize our Data Teams process to continuously support our school mission: *We believe that it is a shared responsibility among Berea's stakeholders to foster positive academic, emotional, social, and physical growth in a nurturing, risk-free environment. Diversity will be celebrated, creating students who respect one another and embrace differences. Through the implementation of the New York State Learning Standards and an aligned curriculum, creative and critical thinkers will meet and exceed school district standards, ensuring future success and life-long learning.*

Although working with a poverty rate of close to 20 percent, this is not a story about a school that suffers through immense poverty, lack of resources, or poor test scores. It is, however, a story about a school that strives for continuous improvement in every aspect of our daily responsibilities. From our custodial staff that designs and analyzes teacher survey data to an office staff that tracks parental involvement via volunteerism and attendance during school-related events, many facets of our professional lives are devoted to finding ways that we can bring out the "Berea Best" in each other and our students.

The Valley Central School District's accountability endeavors began during the 2006/07 school year when a district-wide team of administrators, teachers, and parents began their training in Data Teams, Decision Making for Results, and Common Formative Assessments. Throughout this training period and during preliminary implementation, an awakening occurred in our district. All stakeholders came to realize the importance of collecting and analyzing data in order to drive instruction and create an instructional environment focused on continuous improvement. Building-based needs were determined and goals were developed. In order to continuously support these goals, an array of professional development opportunities have been provided via the building and district levels. These opportunities were created to ensure all Valley Central employees embrace the concept that their job responsibilities, regardless of what they entail, are directly or indirectly tied to student achievement.

Preliminary conversations with school stakeholders revealed building goals created during the 2007/08 school year were superfluous, with minimal connection to our building needs. Teachers and staff were going through the motions without focus on and ownership of the accountability process. This lack of ownership translated to minimal success related to student achievement. With Berea's accountability team responsible for overseeing building progress, we collaborated to present a plan that required staff ownership, coupled with passion for the process. Data Teams were carefully designed to create building goals that addressed genuine building needs. More importantly, these teams were structured in such a manner as to enhance staff ownership in the accountability process. This sense of empowerment inspired staff to create action steps and assessments that specifically addressed building needs, and enabled staff to infuse their specific area of expertise into the Data Teams process. By the end of my first year, Berea's improvement plan revolved around strategic building goals and, more importantly, Data Teams that capitalized on staff strengths and expertise in order to foster a true sense of dedication to and ownership of the accountability process. We were also very proud of our foresight to weave new literacy framework components into our Data Team strategies. Berea's kindergarten and first-grade Data Teams took it a step further and utilized required district literacy assessments as the nexus for both their Data Teams' strategic actions and related formative assessments. Connecting our district literacy framework and required literacy assessments throughout our targeted action steps ensured a sense of sustainability throughout our instructional agenda.

My second year as Berea's leader involved the incorporation of Common Formative Assessments within the accountability process. While all teams were dedicated to this endeavor, I became particularly concerned about the amount of time our fourth-grade Data Team was devoting to the development of Common Formative Assessments yielding intermittent results. This group of motivated professionals spent hours designing these assessments, but soon discovered that, despite their efforts, these assessments were not providing them with the instant data that they required to adjust their instruction. Furthermore, the data generated from their assessments provided abstract results. These professionals were unable to pinpoint specific deficits in order to determine corresponding instructional strategies that addressed student needs. Precious hours and energy had been devoted to the Data Teams process, yet this team was unable to move forward with both timely and targeted instruction that would result in enhanced student achievement. The absence of valid and reliable data began to turn this team's motivation into frustration toward the accountability process.

## DELIBERATE DATA

Concerned with teacher burnout, I turned to Connie Kamm, Senior Professional Development Associate from The Leadership and Learning Center. Connie has consulted for Valley Central stakeholders on our accountability plan implementation since the beginning of the initiative. She has become a mentor to me, as well as an inspiration. During her room service dinner, Connie listened to the concerns I shared regarding my fourth-grade teachers and plainly concurred that this team, in particular, was working too hard, without attaining significant results to lead to sustainable progress. I breathed a sigh of relief as I wholeheartedly agreed. Connie and I then spent the remainder of our phone conversation discussing the concept of deliberate data, along with the strategies we needed to weave into our Data Teams process, while inspiring a collective ownership in this adjusted approach.

During a faculty meeting shortly following the conversation with Connie, I presented the deliberate data concept to my staff. This meeting began as a celebration of the successes we had experienced related to each team's development of action steps, assessments, and overall data collection. After acknowledging their hard work, I genuinely expressed the need to obtain deliberate data, which would result in immediate feedback to strategically adjust instruction. I continued the conversation by reiterating the powerful connection that must exist between assessments and instruction. I recall most of my teachers breathing a similar and collective sigh of relief as I began explaining the deliberate data approach.

A discussion then ensued in order to define a deliberate data approach for our school community. We discussed how data is only useful when it provides educators with ongoing, unequivocal evidence that students are learning. The utilization of deliberate data, tied to building goals, fulfills that prerequisite as it pinpoints a deficit area and coincides with an assessment that provides timely feedback. This feedback provides educators with relevant information that allows them to strategically connect student data to instructional practices. Ultimately, this type of data delivers pertinent information about students' learning needs. Optimally, deliberate data should encompass a monthly summary of data based on a three-week cycle of data collection. Another way to look at it is to take AYP (adequate yearly progress) and make it AMP (adequate monthly progress).

As a follow-up to our deliberate data discussion, Berea's Data Teams met in order to brainstorm ways that deliberate data could be infused into their own Data Team focus and action steps. While some teams recognized their team's focus tied nicely to the deliberate data approach, other teams came to the rapid realization that they needed to make adjustments related to the assessment process tied to their action steps. Our fourth-grade team experienced an epiphany during this discussion and immediately developed a plan that is articulated by Berea teacher Tracey Vianden in the following pages.

Tracey Vianden is a special education teacher in a self-contained class teaching fourth and fifth graders with varying emotional and learning needs. She has high expectations for herself, her students, and her staff, going above and beyond for her students on a daily basis. Stepping into her room, one can immediately feel the care she puts into each one of her lessons. She has mastered the balance of nurturing her students' abilities, while challenging them to overcome the odds in order to reach their full potential.

Tracey is an active member of our fourth-grade Data Team and has firsthand experience of the energy associated with this Data Team's efforts. After the results of the New York State English Language Arts exam were released, Tracey Vianden had a vested interest in the implementation of our deliberate data approach.

In July 2010, we found out that our special education cohort did not make AYP for this exam. The news turned darker when we realized that if our special education cohort did not make AYP during the 2010/11 school year, Berea would be classified as a school in need of improvement. We were devastated. After the disappointment subsided, we decided to turn this news into an opportunity to exercise our all-encompassing goal: continuous improvement.

After poring over the state test data, we came to the very hard realization that getting our special education students to reach proficiency on these exams would require a focused effort. Putting numbers and data aside, we had qualitative information to consider as well. We knew our special education students lacked confidence. They would not take risks across the educational spectrum. Throw in the word "test" and they would give up. Adding to the pressure, test proctors are not allowed to give testing modifications such as words or questions read as needed. Essentially, these students are asked to take a high-stakes test without any of the support that they are accustomed to.

After brainstorming an array of strategies to overcome this challenge, the answer was right in front of our noses. Berea's teachers had recently been trained in Balanced Math (Leadership and Learning Center, 2011) and witnessed tremendous success via the concept of daily (spiral) math reviews. In a nutshell, each teacher presents his students with four or five math problems that encompass our number sense focus tied to our building goal. After the students attempt these problems on their own, teachers review each one as a class and discuss various strategies and approaches for each. The discussion that revolves around these math problems provides immediate data and feedback our teachers use to tailor instruction for future lessons. These reviews allow our teachers to reteach concepts that their students are struggling with and, in turn, efficiently move on to new skills they need to master.

Our fourth-grade team wondered, If this daily review approach works for math, why can't this concept apply to literacy? Tracey Vianden researched a variety of materials and came upon a resource that would meet the instructional deficits as well as boost overall student confidence and engagement in the learning process. Our fourth-grade Data Team couldn't resist and jumped in with "both feet." Here is their story in Tracey Vianden's words . . .

## DATA TEAM SUCCESS STORY

Before Valley Central implemented the Data Teams approach, Berea teachers struggled to come up with a fair and methodical way to measure student achievement. Each teacher worked alone, designing assessments to determine if students met proficiency levels related to taught content and concepts. Little attention was given to these results as teachers robotically moved onto new material with minimal reflection related to our instruction. The assessments were rarely connected to teaching in a manner that would inform instruction. As our Data Teams process unfolded and goals were formulated, my colleagues and I began to collectively design Common Formative Assessments tied to building goals and student learning needs.

For two years, our Data Team created Common Formative Assessments related to Berea's English language arts and math goals. While this process brought us closer to connecting student achievement to future instruction, we struggled to come up with Common Formative Assessments connected to our English language arts goals that provided us with immediate and strategic feedback to adjust our planning. The time span for administering the pre-assessment, collaboratively sharing the data, and discussing targeted instructional strategies was too prolonged to adequately meet the needs of our at-risk population.

While our team struggled to design effective English language arts assessments, we found success in creating Common Formative Assessments related to math, primarily due to our intense number sense focus. As a matter of fact, our mathematical Common Formative Assessments guided the creation of our daily (spiral) math reviews mentioned previously.

Our entire fourth-grade team utilizes the Balanced Math approach. Monday through Thursday, the students complete four teacher-created problems based on concepts they previously learned. These problems are then reviewed during the start of our math lesson. Students who are struggling come in for extra help during study hall and are exposed to strategies matched to their learning needs. On Friday, students are given a weekly test on the concepts that were covered during the week via the Balanced Math review. The skills that remain areas of concern are spiraled into the math review the following week. Because of the success of the Balanced Math approach and the deliberate data we collected, we were inspired to apply this approach to our literacy goals.

Beginning in the fall of 2010, this team applied the math review approach to literacy in the form of the Daily ELA Review. Monday through Thursday, various aspects of instruction are focused on a targeted literacy skill. The targeted skills covered represent the deficit areas depicted on past literacy assessments and include focus areas such as finding the main idea and author's purpose, using context clues, sequencing events, noting details, and making inferences. The students read a passage and answer four questions directly related to the aforementioned skills. Students are provided with only those modifications that are allowed during the New York State English Language Arts assessment to help them prepare for the authentic testing environment that occurs during this assessment. (Ninety percent of Tracey Vianden's students are reading at least two years below grade level, which makes it very difficult for them to complete this task independently.) After the students complete the Daily ELA Review, questions are reviewed as a whole class during our reading time.

More importantly, strategies are discussed on how to pinpoint the correct answers within the text. On Friday, the students are given a passage from a past New York State English Language Arts assessment. This weekly routine has inspired our students to take a chance, as well as provided them with enhanced experience in authentic testing situations. Overall, this approach has given them the confidence that they most truly need to feel successful. Lack of confidence has been an obstacle in the past and an area of concern across the academic spectrum, especially for special education students.

Since September, our fourth-grade Data Team has seen an increase in students' Friday test scores. This data has also provided us with a better understanding of the literacy skills our students need to succeed. The daily reviews, as well as the weekly tests, allow our teaching team to reinforce deficit areas and test-taking strategies in a deliberate manner, giving our students opportunities to revisit and review targeted concepts. The immediate feedback provided by these daily reviews and weekly tests has afforded us the deliberate data we needed to tailor our instruction.

Designing Common Formative Assessments as a Data Team has afforded us the experience to work collectively, guided by clear goals and deliberate evaluations to inform and guide our instruction. This process of using data has empowered our team in immeasurable ways. As a whole, our fourth-grade Data Team is more focused than ever on student learning and achievement. More importantly, we have become reenergized and empowered. We feel the future can only lead us to increased success. We are no longer struggling to create Common Formative Assessments that did not provide the deliberate data needed to immediately adjust our lessons. Instead, we are utilizing data to capture the strengths and needs of our students. This process has allowed us to drive our instruction in the right direction, at a healthy pace for our learners.

## IMPACT OF THE DELIBERATE DATA APPROACH

You can observe from Tracey Vianden's account of her fourth-grade Data Team's success that their desire to meet the instructional needs of their students has propelled them onward and upward. These teachers are data driven and student centered with an overall focus on student success and achievement, as well as continuous improvement. I am very proud of their dedication, devotion, and overall effort to ensure all students reach their full potential.

Tracey Vianden's account did not mention the powerful impact this deliberate data approach has had across Berea's instructional spectrum. Our teachers have witnessed the instructional benefits of the timely feedback associated with this approach. Their Data Team discussions now revolve around new ways they can implement deliberate data in guided reading groups, writing projects, interactive read-aloud activities, and much more. Our teachers are creating checklists and rubrics to obtain necessary feedback to inform future instruction. Another added benefit is that our teachers are sharing this assessment information with our learners. Berea students know the academic expectations prior to the assessment process and understand the results obtained. Both teachers and students then work with each other to formulate individualized goals to support our continuous improvement focus. Teachers and students alike are more aware of the teaching and learning process due to this collaborative approach. This enhanced awareness ensures all stakeholders are lifelong learners with a focus on the future based on real-time results.

Above all, Berea's teachers have evolved into reflective educators. When results are analyzed, our teachers utilize both positive and negative outcomes to develop strategies that address learning needs across the cognitive spectrum. Excuses are not directed at the students as teachers collectively brainstorm strategies to address varied learning deficits. Our teachers own their responsibility in educating our students while keeping the blame game to a minimum.

As for the future, only time will tell. Initial data illustrates an overwhelming sense of accomplishment on behalf of our teachers and students. We are confident that our students will approach state assessments with vigor and confidence due to their experiences with parallel tasks throughout the course of a year. Student engagement has increased in direct relation to the confidence they have in their ability to take risks across the academic spectrum. As a matter of fact, I recently observed Tracey

Vianden's class participating in a Reader's Theatre activity. The enthusiasm and motivation was evident on each student's face. The discussion that ensued after the Reader's Theatre activity was brimming with higher-level thoughts, inquiries, and resolutions, those not typical in a self-contained special education classroom.

The success of the deliberate data endeavors experienced by several of our Data Teams has become a bit contagious. Other teams have heard these success stories and are in the process of refining their own deliberate data strategies and assessments, with an intense focus on student achievement. We are proud of our accomplishments and look forward to future instructional adjustments based on the data we obtain.

While our current accountability plan has only been in place for a little over two years, the teachers and staff at Berea have accomplished a great deal. As a focused team, we are extremely proud of our efforts to determine clear goals that address genuine building needs, while weaving required literacy components and assessments into our action steps. Adding the deliberate data approach to our formative assessment process instantly enables our teachers to witness the results of their efforts. They are able to adjust instruction during the lesson, as opposed to days or even weeks afterward. This approach has become a distinct part of our Data Team discussions and daily instructional interactions as teachers work with and learn from each other to enhance the engagement and achievement of all Berea students. The entire Berea staff is motivated, determined, and focused on continuous improvement in each lesson they deliver and the results that are attained. Everyone benefits from this approach as our teachers are teaching smarter, and challenging our students to reach their full potential. The deliberate data approach has inspired all teachers, students, support staff, and administrators to reach their Berea Best.

| | | | **GETTING REAL...** | | | |

As you reflect on Berea Elementary School's real-time decisions, think about how their story applies to you in your current setting, and then answer the following questions:

1. *"Although working with a poverty rate of close to 20 percent, this is not a story about a school that suffers through immense poverty, lack of resources, or poor test scores. It is, however, a story about a school that strives for continuous improvement in every aspect of our daily respon-sibilities. From our custodial staff that designs and analyzes teacher survey data to an office staff that tracks parental involvement via volunteerism and attendance during school-related events, many facets of our profes-sional lives are devoted to finding ways that we can bring out the 'Berea Best' in each other and our students."*

   Does this level of commitment to improvement exist in every area of your building or district? What, if any, are the trouble spots in making this a reality?

   _____

   _____

   _____

   _____

2. The principal of Berea explains how the school abandoned the concept of only working toward AYP (Adequate Yearly Progress), and that through the implementation of formative assessments the faculty was able to look at AMP (Adequate Monthly Progress). As the chapter progresses, we learn some of her educators have even gotten into the habit of assessing ADP (Adequate Daily Progress).

   Do you currently practice assessment for AYP, AMP, AWP (Adequate Weekly Progress), or ADP? Explain what your assessment routine involves.

   _____

   _____

   _____

   _____

3. After teams have become fluid in the process of administering Common Formative Assessments, they often determine how to take these exams to the next level because of their effectiveness. *"Our fourth-grade team wondered, If this approach works for math, why can't this concept apply to literacy?"*

It is clear formative assessment is a scientific process. It involves deep learning, thinking, application, reflection, and modifications. What other specific evidence do you see throughout the chapter that reflects this notion?

_____

_____

_____

_____

4. *"Another added benefit is that our teachers are sharing this assessment information with our learners. Berea students know the academic expectations prior to the assessment process and understand the results obtained. Both teachers and students then work with each other to formulate individualized goals to support our continuous improvement focus."*

Are you (or your teachers) sharing real-time data from frequent assessments with your students, and working with them to set individualized goals?

_____

_____

_____

_____

# CHAPTER NINE

# Ocean View Elementary School
## Norfolk, Virginia

*"We started using student common assessment data to evaluate not only student proficiency, but also the effectiveness of our instructional and intervention program."*

—Lauren Campsen, Principal

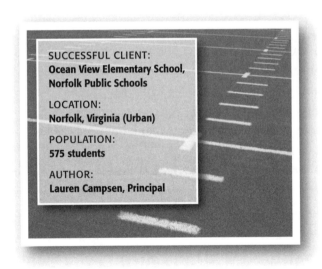

SUCCESSFUL CLIENT:
**Ocean View Elementary School, Norfolk Public Schools**

LOCATION:
**Norfolk, Virginia (Urban)**

POPULATION:
**575 students**

AUTHOR:
**Lauren Campsen, Principal**

# BACKGROUND

Ocean View Elementary School in Norfolk, Virginia, entered the new century during the 1999/2000 school year with a new principal, low student achievement levels (as measured by the State of Virginia Standards of Learning accountability tests), and no state accreditation. The school faced many of the same challenges encountered by urban public schools across the nation. The school, built in 1939, had little new technology and, never renovated, inadequate electrical capacity to support upgrades. The paint peeled off the walls, the roof leaked, and the building was dark and dingy. Students came from low-socioeconomic and working-class homes, many single parent or grandparent led. Much of the population was transient. A shelter for homeless, mother-led families was two blocks from the school. Booming construction in the city and a Catholic church with the only Spanish mass in the area drew an increasing number of Central American Hispanic immigrants (many illegal and not speaking English) to the neighborhood. A culture of acceptance of the status quo pervaded the school. The perception among many staff members was that "these" children simply could not learn. Low student achievement became a self-fulfilling prophecy. The time for change had come.

Today, a decade later, the roof on Ocean View School still leaks, but long ropes of cable carry electricity to fuel the computers and smart boards in the classrooms. Paint still peels from the walls and the school still waits for its turn for renovation, but colorful banners and bulletin boards filled with student work brighten its hallways. When students are nonproficient, teachers no longer blame school demographics, but instead take a brave look in the mirror to find the cause and then focus on developing strategies to change student performance. Each morning students are reminded that they attend a National No Child Left Behind Blue Ribbon School, a three-time Virginia Distinguished Title I School, and, this year, a Virginia School of Excellence. Ask any Ocean View student what kind of school he goes to and he'll tell you a "world-class school."

Exhibits 9.1 through 9.4 show the track of the evolution of Ocean View Elementary School from low performing and unaccredited in 2000 to high performing and nationally recognized in 2010.

# PARADIGM SHIFTS AND CHALLENGES

Ocean View's transformation from low performing to high performing was dependent on overcoming three major challenges. First, administrators and teachers needed to make a paradigm shift in their fundamental beliefs. They needed to stop blaming demographics, students, and parents for low student achievement. Instead,

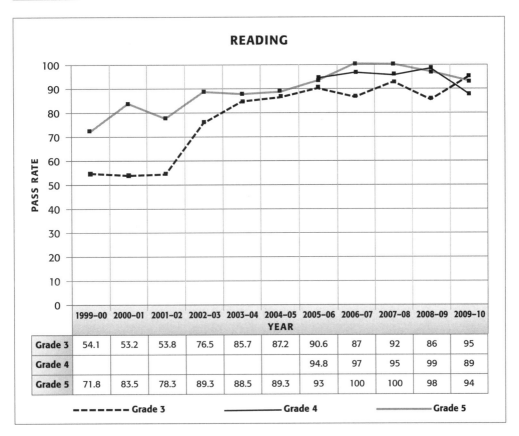

**EXHIBIT 9.1** Ocean View Elementary School Percentage of Students Scoring Proficient or Higher in Reading, Virginia Standards of Learning Tests, 2000–2010

|         | 1999–00 | 2000–01 | 2001–02 | 2002–03 | 2003–04 | 2004–05 | 2005–06 | 2006–07 | 2007–08 | 2008–09 | 2009–10 |
|---------|---------|---------|---------|---------|---------|---------|---------|---------|---------|---------|---------|
| Grade 3 | 54.1    | 53.2    | 53.8    | 76.5    | 85.7    | 87.2    | 90.6    | 87      | 92      | 86      | 95      |
| Grade 4 |         |         |         |         |         |         | 94.8    | 97      | 95      | 99      | 89      |
| Grade 5 | 71.8    | 83.5    | 78.3    | 89.3    | 88.5    | 89.3    | 93      | 100     | 100     | 98      | 94      |

– – – – – – Grade 3          ——————— Grade 4          ——————— Grade 5

every professional in the school needed to accept personal accountability for the achievement of each and every child (a brave look in the mirror). Second, all students at each grade level needed to be evaluated on the same material using the same assessment (Power Standards and Common Formative Assessments). Third, the student achievement data from these assessments, rather than tossed on a shelf and forgotten, needed to be used to inform planning and instruction (data-driven decision making).

# THE EXPERTS:
# RESEARCH AND PROFESSIONAL DEVELOPMENT

Early in the decade, Norfolk Public Schools brought in a number of nationally recognized professionals in education to address student achievement. Two of these

**EXHIBIT 9.2** **Ocean View Elementary School Percentage of Students Scoring Proficient or Higher in Math, Virginia Standards of Learning Tests, 2000–2010**

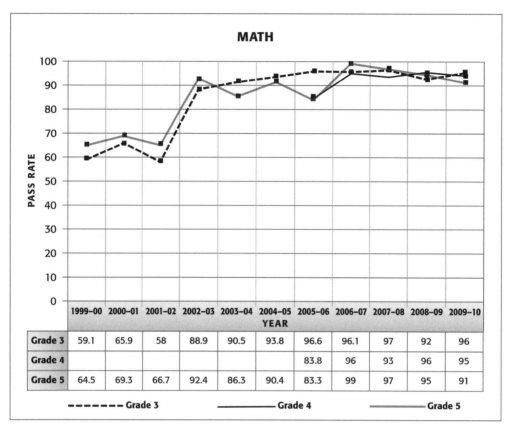

| | 1999–00 | 2000–01 | 2001–02 | 2002–03 | 2003–04 | 2004–05 | 2005–06 | 2006–07 | 2007–08 | 2008–09 | 2009–10 |
|---|---|---|---|---|---|---|---|---|---|---|---|
| Grade 3 | 59.1 | 65.9 | 58 | 88.9 | 90.5 | 93.8 | 96.6 | 96.1 | 97 | 92 | 96 |
| Grade 4 | | | | | | | 83.8 | 96 | 93 | 96 | 95 |
| Grade 5 | 64.5 | 69.3 | 66.7 | 92.4 | 86.3 | 90.4 | 83.3 | 99 | 97 | 95 | 91 |

------ Grade 3          ———— Grade 4          ════ Grade 5

experts, Douglas Reeves and Larry Ainsworth, became the inspiration for all the hard work that led to key changes at Ocean View.

As the new principal of one of the district's low-performing schools, I was determined to find a way to turn our school around. After listening to a keynote address by Douglas Reeves in which he addressed the issue of accountability in education, I bought and read his book *Accountability in Action* (2000). In this book, he shared the four key components of an effective accountability system: student achievement, school performance, ways to help students learn, and (my "Aha") determining educational effectiveness. I can honestly say that this was a transforming moment for me as an educator. Commitment to the concept that a school and its instructional program is THE key to student achievement, regardless of school demographics, is the foundation for all that has happened to Ocean View Elementary School in the past decade.

**EXHIBIT 9.3** Ocean View Elementary School Percentage of Students Scoring Proficient or Higher in Science, Virginia Standards of Learning Tests, 2000–2010

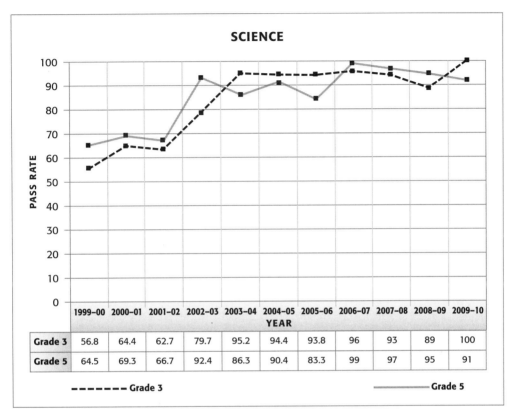

| | 1999–00 | 2000–01 | 2001–02 | 2002–03 | 2003–04 | 2004–05 | 2005–06 | 2006–07 | 2007–08 | 2008–09 | 2009–10 |
|---|---|---|---|---|---|---|---|---|---|---|---|
| Grade 3 | 56.8 | 64.4 | 62.7 | 79.7 | 95.2 | 94.4 | 93.8 | 96 | 93 | 89 | 100 |
| Grade 5 | 64.5 | 69.3 | 66.7 | 92.4 | 86.3 | 90.4 | 83.3 | 99 | 97 | 95 | 91 |

- - - - - - Grade 3                                          ——————— Grade 5

That summer of 2001, when I heard that our district was sending a group of interested principals to Douglas Reeves' Center for Performance Assessment (now The Leadership and Learning Center) in Denver, Colorado, for a week of training in data-driven decision making, I asked to be included. Certainly, like most teachers, I had often used some student achievement data to occasionally make instructional decisions in my own classroom. But the idea that an entire school, or even a school district, could systematically use student assessment and achievement data to drive ALL planning and instructional decisions was a revelation. That week's professional development in learning how to do this became the springboard for school change at Ocean View. I began reading *Making Standards Work* (2002b), also by Douglas Reeves, on the plane ride home. A vision for school improvement was forming.

**Ocean View Elementary School Percentage of Students Scoring Proficient or Higher in Social Studies, Virginia Standards of Learning Tests, 2000–2010**

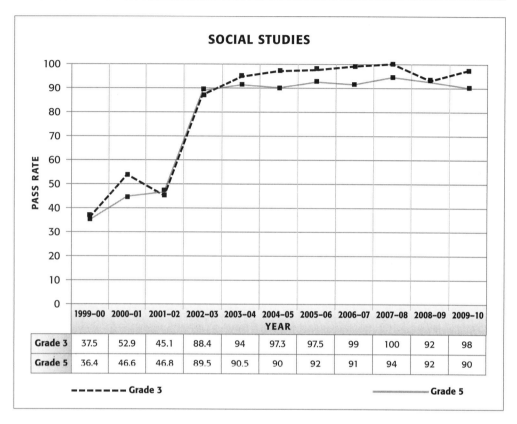

| | 1999-00 | 2000-01 | 2001-02 | 2002-03 | 2003-04 | 2004-05 | 2005-06 | 2006-07 | 2007-08 | 2008-09 | 2009-10 |
|---|---|---|---|---|---|---|---|---|---|---|---|
| **Grade 3** | 37.5 | 52.9 | 45.1 | 88.4 | 94 | 97.3 | 97.5 | 99 | 100 | 92 | 98 |
| **Grade 5** | 36.4 | 46.6 | 46.8 | 89.5 | 90.5 | 90 | 92 | 91 | 94 | 92 | 90 |

- - - - - - Grade 3                                    ——————— Grade 5

# 2001/02:
# THE FIRST YEAR—CHALLENGES AND LESSONS LEARNED

The new school year started with the distribution of loose-leaf notebooks and section dividers to all classroom teachers. Each grade-level team was asked to list all state, district, and class assessments and tests (we didn't have school-wide common assessments yet) and make a tab in their new notebooks for storing the data from each one. Requiring teachers to actually put their data reports into these notebooks, instead of in a file drawer, and meeting with me to review the data turned out to be the first of many time-consuming challenges. Trying to focus discussions at meetings with the site-based management team on student instruction and achievement (rather than teacher dress codes and how to divvy up school funds) proved to be the next one. Finally, identifying exactly how to use the data we were collecting and what kind of assessment data we still needed to determine student mastery of state standards became ongoing questions for us.

Once again, my district, Norfolk Public Schools, came to the rescue—they brought in a new expert. School principals, accompanied by one teacher, were invited to a multiday workshop on "'Unwrapping' the Standards." There, under the guidance of Larry Ainsworth, my school reading specialist and I found answers to our questions about exactly what kind of student assessment data we needed and, even, how to create it ourselves. We looked at Virginia's Standards of Learning for each grade level. We practiced ways for identifying which standards had the most leverage for student success—the Power Standards. We learned how to break down ("unwrap") each Power Standard to determine the concepts and skills students would need to know in order to master the standard. Finally, we were given guidelines for actually writing our own Common Formative Assessments (CFAs), so that we could begin to link state standards to our school assessments. Using that assessment data to inform instructional planning and implementation would complete the linking of standards to instruction to assessment. But, how could we make that happen?

At our next staff meeting, using an idea from Larry Ainsworth, each grade level was asked to list the 10 most important math skills a student needed to be successful in math when they entered their grade in September. Then teams met with their feeder grade to share their list. Together they reviewed the state standards and matched the standards to their first list, revising their list as needed. Our first Power Standards were created! We repeated this procedure with reading, science, and social studies. Then, volunteers began meeting at school on Saturdays to write short, 10-question common monthly assessments aligned to each Power Standard. It was slow going and hard, especially since only a handful of teachers were doing the bulk of the work. However, we finished a few initial common assessments and piloted them in the spring.

By the end of that school year, we had become very good at collecting and organizing student data in our shiny new notebooks. Power Standards had been developed in all subjects in each grade and put into a monthly sequence. We had even written and administered a few common assessments. Most of us had worked very hard. But our proficiency scores on the state accountability tests that year didn't budge; instead they remained disappointingly low. It was a dark time. To some, the test scores proved their belief that our students couldn't learn. They simply wouldn't believe that the failure was ours. But I knew the failure was mine. My vision for a high-performing school, where student achievement could never be predicted by demographics, was possible for Ocean View Elementary School. But my implementation of the necessary changes was too slow and too weak.

The summer of 2002 brought new opportunities for more professional development and an opportunity to build on the foundation laid the previous year. Norfolk

Public Schools again sent a group of administrators to The Center. This time the training was in developing Data Teams to analyze student assessment data, indentify nonproficient students, and develop instructional intervention strategies. Flying home from Denver, I thought about Douglas Reeves' words, *"It is, therefore, essential that the principal indentify faculty leaders who have already accepted the principle that standards-based education is appropriate, important, and vital to the health of our schools. Take some time to nurture these leaders, and ensure that they share a common vision with you"* (Reeves 2000). I knew what I needed to do.

## 2002/03:
## THE SECOND YEAR—MORE HARD WORK BRINGS SUCCESS

When I returned to school, I contacted a group of teachers who had embraced my vision for Ocean View and worked hard the previous year to implement our changes. Tony Flach (then employed by Norfolk Public Schools, but also certified by The Center as an instructor in both data-driven decision making and Data Teams) came to our school and guided this newly formed leadership group. Together, these dedicated teachers and I developed a new leadership model around Data Teams. The reading specialist would lead a vertical English Data Team. The newly appointed math resource teacher would lead a vertical mathematics Data Team. Two classroom teachers would lead vertical science and social studies Data Teams. New grade-level team leaders were selected to lead horizontal grade-level Data Teams. A team member from each grade level was assigned to each vertical team. The vertical team leaders, the school counselor, and the special education team leader, along with the principal, formed the newly created Lead Data Team. Once created, our newly formed Data Teams needed student data to analyze. The hard work of writing monthly common assessments for each Power Standard began.

Using the blueprint provided during the workshop with Larry Ainsworth, initial monthly assessments were developed and administered throughout the school year. Grade-level Data Teams met and analyzed their monthly data, then took the information to their content vertical teams, where school-wide patterns were identified and instructional strategies developed for each grade in each subject. The information was used by classroom teachers to guide intervention lessons for nonproficient students. Next, the Lead Data Team met the first Friday of each month to review the vertical team reports and identify specific teachers in need of support. Resource teachers were repositioned to provide assistance to these teachers and their students. Monthly assessment data was charted on large graphs outside each classroom, and grade-level teams met with the principal to discuss their data and to encourage

An Ocean View Data Team meets to review student data from a Common Formative Assessment.

teachers with high proficiency rates to share strategies with team members whose classes had not performed to standard. In addition, administration of STAR Reading and STAR Math to check student grade level in reading and math, previously given in September and May, was extended to a third administration in January to better measure student improvement. This was the beginning of using student common assessment data to evaluate not only student proficiency, but also the effectiveness of our instructional and intervention program.

The 2002/03 school year became the pivotal year in Ocean View's transformational journey. Most Ocean View teachers embraced the changes, eager to find new ways to help their students. They gave generously of their time in the afternoons and on Saturdays to help write assessments and plan together to develop strategies. We began to survey effective teaching research looking for best practices and discovered Robert Marzano and *Classroom Instruction That Works* (Marzano, Pickering, and Pollock, 2001). We began implementing the strategies from the book in our daily classroom and intervention instruction. These wonderful, dedicated teachers were on a mission to save the world's children starting with Ocean View. But other teachers dug in with hard resistance, remaining mute during mandatory data meetings, refusing to share or plan with teammates, and throwing up roadblocks to implementations whenever possible. They didn't want their data posted and were insulted that I could suggest that their instruction could possibly be the reason for low student achievement in their class. They questioned every strategy and every procedure. The answer to each challenging question became our school mantra: "Are we accredited yet?" Some requested transfers at the end of the year, while others remained to fight another day. The rest of us waited for the state assessment data to be released.

At the end of a sunny day in June—Field Day at Ocean View—we received a phone call that the SOL (Virginia Standards of Learning) Tests' raw data was being released on the Internet. Fifth-grade teachers sat in my office with calculators, averaging proficiency rates for each subject in their classes as I counted the number of students in each room that had made a passing score of 400 or better on the tests. Third-grade teachers sat in the assistant principal's office next door doing the same. In 2003, we needed to have 70 percent of our students pass each test to earn accreditation. Except for fifth-grade reading and writing, we had never reached this benchmark in any subject. In fact, we had been unable to reach 50 percent in science and social studies and had not been able to reach even 55 percent proficiency in third-grade reading. We literally sat in shock as teachers began to shout out their proficiency percentages. We had 20 and 30 point jumps on many tests, with most over 80 percent and none under 70 percent. Our hard work had paid off. Our belief in our students to learn and in ourselves to change our school had worked. State accreditation was ours! One teacher, who had resisted the whole year, looked at me and said, "My god, all those things you made us do actually worked." I still get butterflies in my stomach remembering that comment. On a visit to Norfolk, Doug Reeves once told us, "The data will give you the buy-in." And so it did. No year to come would ever be as hard or as exciting as the year we had just finished.

The 2002/03 school year was also the first year for No Child Left Behind and AYP. We learned later that summer that we did not make AYP that first year. Our special education students, exempted from the reading test, had lowered our participation percentages to below 95 percent. It was now time to start looking at our subgroups and, even, individual student performance.

## 2003–2007:
## NEW CHALLENGES WITH ACHIEVEMENT GAPS

Ocean View started the 2003/04 school year with a big celebration of our newly earned state accreditation. Once the party was over, we knew we needed to roll up our sleeves and get back to work. Failure to make AYP forced us to revisit what we were doing with our special education students. Also, 80 percent proficiency rates meant that 20 percent of our students were still not mastering state standards. It was time to look at the performance of our subgroups. The Lead Data Team began to disaggregate our state test data by race and socioeconomic status. Although the low to middle socioeconomic gaps were in single digits, African American–Caucasian achievement gaps across grade levels and content areas were all in double digits, peaking at 22 percent in fifth-grade science. As successful as we had been in increasing overall student achievement, it was obvious that our instruction and intervention program was still not meeting the needs of certain populations of our students. AYP had done its job and put a spotlight on the performance of our subgroups. This revelation led to major additions to Ocean View's instructional program.

Although we were already using monthly common assessment data to check for the effectiveness of classroom instruction, we had no way to check for the effectiveness of the interventions that our nonproficient students were receiving. We decided that what we needed to do was to retest students who did not pass the monthly assessment with another assessment after they received intervention lessons. We named our current monthly assessments Form A and started the task of writing a second assessment for each Power Standard that we named Form B, which was designed to be administered only to those students who had not passed the Form A assessment after they received intervention lessons. We also began to break down each 10-question assessment and list each student who had missed each question so that each intervention lesson was tightly focused on a single subskill of the Power Standard and delivered only to students who were nonproficient on a particular question.

Next, we realized that we needed to look at individual student common assessment results in each class rather than just looking at total class and school results. Instead of waiting until the state test to see how our subgroups were performing, we began to disaggregate our monthly common assessment data. The school counselor was assigned the task of tracking the monthly performance of our African American and Hispanic students. The special education team leader and the ESL teacher were tasked with tracking their students. Class lists for all students were also collected. All this information came to the Lead Data Team. By looking at each of our students individually, we were able to identify struggling students and prioritize them for intervention support. We starting giving these students a second double-dose lesson each day, especially in reading and math.

Poor performance on Form B common assessments given to nonproficient students next drew our attention even more closely to classroom instruction. A massive effort was launched to develop learning activities around the research-based instructional strategies in *A Handbook for Classroom Instruction That Works* (Marzano, et al., 2001) and help teachers use them daily during classroom and intervention instruction. State SOL money was used exclusively to hire part-time retired teachers to provide an additional layer of intervention for low-performing students. This combination of tracking individual student performance, adding part-time intervention teachers for additional layers of intervention, and implementing research-based instructional strategies led to success in closing the African American–Caucasian achievement gap to single digits by 2007 in all grades and subjects. At this point, Ocean View proficiency rates on the state accountability tests had moved above 90 percent. We had learned that the secret to making progress toward our goal of universal proficiency was two pronged. First, we needed to use the student data from our common assessments to identify nonproficient students and provide increasing layers of intervention support using research-based instructional strategies. We also needed to use this data to determine the effectiveness of our classroom and intervention instruction and remain open to making changes in what we were doing.

## 2007–2010:
## SUSTAINABILITY AND SEGUEING INTO
## RESPONSE TO INTERVENTION

We entered the 2007/08 school year with rapidly narrowing achievement gaps and proficiency rates on state testing consistently above 90 percent. We were proud of the results of all of our hard work, but what about that last 5 to 10 percent of our students who stubbornly remained nonproficient? With the occasional drop in proficiency rates—in 2009, third-grade reading dipped below 90 percent to 86 percent—sustainability concerns joined our discussion. Around this time, I started hearing a buzz about Response to Intervention (RTI) at various conferences I was attending and started doing a little more research. To my surprise, I discovered a school organizational model based on using student assessment data to inform instructional planning and implementation very similar to the one we had developed at Ocean View. We already had most of the key RTI components in place—Universal Screening: STAR and PALS testing three times a year; Progress Monitoring: common monthly assessments with data used to guide instruction and interventions; research-based instructional strategies, with a focus on using Marzano's research; and tiered interventions: our double and triple doses of intervention. We adopted RTI language and added the additional RTI structure in Tier 3 that allows us to better serve our lowest-performing nonproficient regular education students. Ocean View is now much more systematic when looking at nonproficient students, and moving them through each tier of intervention, while constantly monitoring the impact of each lesson on student performance.

# SUMMARY

Ocean View Elementary School's decade-long journey from a low-performing to a high-performing school has been marked with hard work and dedication. Over the past 10 years, we have kept a sharp focus on research into effective schools and used that research as a road map to school improvement. The work of Douglas Reeves in accountability and data-driven decision making, Larry Ainsworth in Common Formative Assessments, and Robert Marzano in effective instructional strategies have served as the centerpieces in the transformation of our school. At Ocean View, we know that demographics should never determine or even predict student achievement. We also understand that until we can consistently have 100 percent of our students proficient, our work will not be done. And, so, Ocean View's journey continues . . .

## | | | | GETTING REAL . . . | | | |

As you reflect on Ocean View Elementary School's real-time decisions, think about how their story applies to you in your current setting, and then answer the following questions:

1. Instead of blaming student demographics for the lack of success in previous years at Ocean View, the faculty chose to turn inward and determine a series of actions within their circle of control they knew would lead to increased student achievement. The following statement illustrates one of these real-time decisions: *"[We decided] all students at each grade level needed to be evaluated on the same material using the same assessment (Power Standards and Common Formative Assessments)."*

   Not all educators believe all children should be assessed and taught at the same level. Do the teachers in your setting believe all children should be measured by the same standard? What evidence supports this conclusion?

   _____

   _____

   _____

   _____

2. *"I can honestly say that this was a transforming moment for me as an educator. Commitment to the concept that a school and its instructional program is THE key to student achievement, regardless of school demographics."*

   Do you agree with the concept this principal committed to, that the quality of instruction is the decisive element in academic success? Why or why not?

   _____

   _____

   _____

   _____

3. *"We literally sat in shock as teachers began to shout out their proficiency percentages. We had 20 and 30 point jumps on many tests, with most over 80 percent and none under 70 percent. Our hard work had paid off. Our belief in our students to learn and in ourselves to change our school had worked. State accreditation was ours!"*

   Have you ever experienced this type of triumph after adversity in your setting? If so, what were the events that lead to your results? If not, what did Ocean View Elementary do differently between 2001 and 2003 that lead to being accredited?

   _____

   _____

   _____

   _____

4. Ocean View has had a long and deliberate journey to achieving the results they have realized. Are the 10 years, the trials, and the frustrations worth it in your eyes? Would you have done anything differently? Explain.

   _____

   _____

   _____

   _____

# Conclusion

The average secondary teacher loses anywhere from 5 to 15 minutes of instruction per 45- to 60-minute period. This loss of time can be attributed to taking attendance, students trickling in after the bell, off-task behavior, visitors, classroom movement (including turning in papers, organizing into groups, and so on), and a host of other disruptions. These patterns can result in a loss of 900 to 2,700 instructional minutes per school year for one group of students in one subject, or a decrease of approximately 15 to 45 hours of learning time annually.

For every potential problem, an equally viable solution should be identified. Given the circumstances outlined in the preceding paragraph, schools can be lead to consider adding additional minutes or hours to the day and/or year. However, as Robert Marzano has discovered in his investigations, *"Little research evidence exists to suggest that increasing the school day or school year will increase student achievement. Rather, the crucial issue seems to be how the time is used, with quality of instruction being the key"* (Marzano, 2000). Therefore, we can be confident that the quality of instructional time is at least as important, if not more important, than the quantity.

This then begs the question, how do teachers and school leaders make the most of the time they have? One necessary step we must all take is to learn to acquire the mind-set and discipline to stop doing those things that do not yield the extraordinary results our students require. Many educators employ a multitude of best practices in their classrooms and buildings; however, they often water these efforts down by expending time and energy on those behaviors that do not increase student achievement.

In addition, we must build up the courage to utilize powerful instructional practices even when it is not always comfortable to do so. Where would you rather spend your precious instructional minutes? Managing and implementing the initiative of the day, or leveraging a proven process, like the use of frequent formative assessment that is backed by decades of research, and over time changes student lives and teacher practice leading to high-yield results?

The accounts you read and reflected upon in this book highlight educators who made the choice to maximize their instructional minutes. Their journeys were not easy, and no "silver bullets" were involved, but they understood the real-time power of formative assessment and were willing to take the risk and run the course.

A research study conducted by Leahy and colleagues identifies the changes that occur in educators when they implement formative assessment in their classrooms, and highlights the new behaviors/practices they adopt alongside their students as a result:

> *Teachers using assessment for learning continually look for ways in which they can generate evidence of student learning, and they use this evidence to adapt their instruction to better meet their students' learning needs. They share the responsibility for learning with the learners; students know that they are responsible for alerting the teacher when they do not understand. Teachers design their instruction to yield evidence about student achievement; for example, they carefully craft hinge-point questions to create "moments of contingency," in which the direction of the instruction will depend on student responses. Teachers provide feedback that engages students, make time in class for students to work on improvement, and activate students as instructional resources for one another.* (Leahy, Lyon, Thompson, and Wiliam, 2005)

Take a moment to reflect on the current status of your classroom, school, or district. Are the practices outlined by these researchers evident in your setting? If not, what is preventing you or your faculty from implementing them? Perhaps the summary of this research will be an encouragement to you:

> *All this sounds like a lot of work, but according to our teachers, **it doesn't take any more time than the practices they used to engage in.** And these techniques are far more effective. Teachers tell us that they are enjoying their teaching more.* (Leahy, Lyon, Thompson, and Wiliam, 2005; emphasis added)

It is my hope, and the hope of the leaders featured in this book, that you would utilize every instructional minute you are afforded to benefit your professional practice, that the needs of your students would drive you to begin operating as they require, and that you would provide each other with the immediate feedback that will create changes in the way we teach and the way we learn. This is real-time instruction!

I implore you to spend your instructional minutes attending to what matters most! The words of Carl Sandburg are an accurate reflection of all these thoughts: *"Time is the coin of your life. It is the only coin you have, and only you can determine how it will be spent."*

# References

Ainsworth, L. (2003a). *Power standards: Identifying the standards that matter the most.* Englewood, CO: Lead + Learn Press.

Ainsworth, L. (2003b). *"Unwrapping" the standards: A simple process to make standards manageable.* Englewood, CO: Lead + Learn Press.

Ainsworth, L. (2007). Common formative assessments: The centerpiece of an integrated standards-based assessment system. In D. Reeves (Ed.), *Ahead of the curve: The power of assessment to transform teaching and learning* (pp. 78–101). Bloomington, IN: Solution Tree.

Ainsworth, L., & Viegut, D. J. (2006). *Common formative assessments: How to connect standards-based instruction and assessment.* Thousand Oaks, CA: Corwin Press.

Almeida, L., & Ainsworth, L. (2009). *Engaging classroom assessments: The making standards work series.* Englewood, CO: Lead + Learn Press.

Black, P., & Wiliam, D. (1998, October). Inside the black box: Raising standards through classroom assessment. *Phi Delta Kappan, 80*(2), 139–144, 146–148.

Brookhart, S. (1996). *How to give effective feedback to your students.* Alexandria, VA: ASCD.

Carter, L. (2007). *Total instructional alignment: From standards to student success.* Bloomington, IN: Solution Tree.

Davies, A. (2007). Involving students in the classroom assessment process. In D. Reeves (Ed.), *Ahead of the curve: The power of assessment to transform teaching and learning* (pp. 30–57). Bloomington, IN: Solution Tree.

Deming, W. E. (1982). *Out of Crisis.* Cambridge, MA: MIT Press.

DuFour, R., & Eaker, R. (1998). *Professional learning communities at work: Best practices for enhancing student achievement.* Bloomington, IN: Solution Tree.

Hattie, J. (2009). *Visible learning: A synthesis of over 800 meta-analyses relating to achievement.* London: Routledge.

Leadership and Learning Center, The. (2006). *Common formative assessments.* 1st ed. Englewood, CO: Lead + Learn Press.

Leadership and Learning Center, The. (2008). *Decision making for results.* Englewood, CO: Lead + Learn Press.

Leadership and Learning Center, The. (2010). *Data teams.* 3rd ed. Englewood, CO: Lead + Learn Press.

Leadership and Learning Center, The. (2011). *Five easy steps to a balanced math program.* 2nd ed. Englewood, CO: Lead + Learn Press.

Leahy, S., Lyon, C., Thompson, M., & Wiliam, D. (2005). Classroom assessment: Minute by minute, day by day. *Educational Leadership, 63*(3), 19–24.

Marzano, R. J. (2000). *A new era of school reform: Going where the research takes us.* Aurora, CO: Mid-continent Research for Education and Learning.

Marzano, R. J. (2003). *What works in schools: Translating research into action.* Alexandria, VA: Association for Supervision and Curriculum Development.

Marzano, R. J., Norford, J. S., Paynter, D. E., Pickering, D. J., & Gaddy, B. B. (2001). *A handbook for classroom instruction that works.* Alexandria, VA: Association for Supervision and Curriculum Development.

Marzano, R. J., Pickering, D. J., & Pollock, J. E. (2001). *Classroom instruction that works.* Alexandria, VA: Association for Supervision and Curriculum Development.

Mississippi Department of Education (MDE). (2007). Curriculum frameworks. Retrieved from http://www.mde.k12.ms.us/ACAD/ID/Curriculum/Curr.htm

OECD. (2005). *Formative assessment: Improving learning in secondary classrooms.* Retrieved from http://www.oecd.org/LongAbstract/0,2546,en_2649_33723_34340421_1_1_1_1,00.html

Popham, W. J. (2003). *Test better, teach better: The instructional role of assessment.* Alexandria, VA: Association for Supervision and Curriculum Development.

Popham, W. J. (2008). *Transformative assessment.* Alexandria, VA: Association for Supervision and Curriculum Development.

Reeves, D. B. (2000). *Accountability in action: A blueprint for learning organizations.* Englewood, CO: Lead + Learn Press.

Reeves, D. B. (2002a). *The leader's guide to standards: A blueprint for educational equity and excellence.* San Francisco, CA: Jossey-Bass.

Reeves, D. B. (2002b). *Making standards work: How to implement standards-based assessments in the classroom, school, and district.* 3rd ed. Englewood, CO: Lead + Learn Press.

Reeves, D. B. (2008). *Reframing teacher leadership to improve your school.* Alexandria, VA: Association for Supervision and Curriculum Development.

Sadler, R. (1989). Formative assessment in the design of instructional systems. *Instructional Science, 18*, 119–144.

Stiggins, R. (2002). Assessment crisis: The absence of assessment FOR learning. *Phi Delta Kappan, 83*(10), 758–765.

Stiggins, R. (2004). From formative assessment to assessment for learning: A path to success in standards-based schools. *Phi Delta Kappan, 87*(4), 324–328.

Stiggins, R. (2007). Assessment for learning: An essential foundation of productive instruction. In D. Reeves (Ed.), *Ahead of the curve: The power of assessment to transform teaching and learning* (pp. 58–76). Bloomington, IN: Solution Tree.